T0137570

LIFE IN THE FRINGES

David de Tremaudan

Order this book online at www.trafford.com
or email orders@trafford.com

Most Trafford titles are also available at major online book retailers.

Printed in the United States of America.

ISBN: 978-1-4269-6021-5 (sc)
ISBN: 978-1-4269-6022-2 (hc)
ISBN: 978-1-4269-6023-9 (e)

Library of Congress Control Number: 2011903455

Trafford rev. 03/03/2011

 www.trafford.com

North America & international
toll-free: 1 888 232 4444 (USA & Canada)
phone: 250 383 6864 ♦ fax: 812 355 4082

LIFE IN THE FRINGES

Table of Contents

INTRODUCTION

Do not read these stories without first reading this introduction. If one does not understand the references made in these stories, it could possibly detract from the "gist" of the story told. One of the most prevalent references is to the "fringes". My reference to this is how society actually views classes of people. We try to look at North America as a class free society, but truth is to those that dwell within these cliques and classes it is all too apparent. Especially to the disenfranchised, the working poor, and so many others that fall beneath the standard of the middle classes. These are the people that sit on the "fringes" of society. They are sometimes viewed with trepidation, tolerance at times, seem to be the "butt" of a joke all to often, and not generally trusted by what could be considered main stream society or what I referred to earlier as the middle classes. These were the ones that fringe dwellers most come in contact with and from whose hand they suffer the worst.

Now I'm not saying that all the stories reflect this sentiment as some stories are outside of this interactional purview, but if you read all of the stories with the perspective of one from the fringes, it puts a whole different spin on things. Give it a try. Too often we only get to see life from that one narrow viewpoint that we were born into. What I try to offer in these short stories as a different perspective. I think it was Harper Lee in her immortal work "To Kill A Mockingbird" that stated, "You can't understand a person until you put his shoes on and walk around in them". Well, here are my shoes, see how they fit.

Short Stories

MEMORIES

The best way to begin this thing is to go back to my earliest memory of note. There are other memories, but not as cohesive and certainly not so significant as this. I have put this one off as a part of my life that others may find as unbelievable and I do want this to be a believable work of non-fiction. At the time there was no real way to measure what my life was, as I had no real yardstick with which to scale it. What I did know was that I had rheumatic fever, I was in a hospital, my roommate was a small boy with horrible burns on his legs, and when I stood at the end of my bed, my chin would come to the top of the end board. I could look out the window at that point and see the dairy down below. I would watch every morning as the white horses were hooked to the wagons and then they would leave every morning on their appointment with whatever destiny that awaited them. I could not fathom too much more than this, because I wasn't tall enough to see more from my window. It 1954 and was I was only 18 months old.

It's kind of hard to say just when it was that I started to remember, but the closest that I can equate it too is waking up and being awake ever since. All of the other memories that come before that, although clear, seem more like lucid dreams. Visiting my grandparents place, playing with my older cousins and brothers, watching my Grandfather working around the barn doing various chores that seemed needing to be done and most of this from my mothers' knee with the surreal affectation of a dream. The morning I woke up in that hospital, there were no more dreams of that nature and I've been cognizant of my surroundings since. At that time I can honestly say that the world around me, which was very small, fascinated me and held my fascination to this day. Naturally, it never remained very small, my little world turned into an ever-expanding universe, and that was just fine by me. When I look back on this time and my fascination with life and its works, a quote of a famous writer and philosopher comes to mind, "Man, armed with his senses sets out to explore the universe and calls the adventure science". I don't know if what I did could be construed as empirical study, but it certainly has been an adventure. But before I digress into witless semantics and ramblings, back to what the story was about.

The last of the milk wagons had just pulled out toward whatever appointments they were to meet and I knew that the lady in white would be back with a trolley loaded with little cups containing all kinds of coloured and odd shaped things. They mostly tasted bad if you tried to chew them. You would take them one by one, pop them into your mouth, and wash them down with a bit of juice. The woman in the white dress, the nurse I guess, would babble at you saying things in baby talk that did little more than embarrass me for her. She would make the most ridiculous faces that one could imagine while she was trying to get you to swallow whatever it was that she was trying to get you to swallow. In retrospect, this was always what I appreciated most about my folks. They always treated you as if you owned a brain. This was not something that most other adults would give kids credit for, so most speak to kids as though their mentally challenged adults. Someone should have told the nurse that we were born with brains, but I guess that wasn't part of her training.

The horses were gone for the day, the nurses had made their rounds, and there was nothing left to do but wait. During these times I would retreat into a world that seemed to have been created for me where I could go to a place that resembled my Grandfathers home. It was a warm place of sunlight and farm animals with sights sounds and smells to go with them. It was a wonderful place and was far away from the nurses, cribs, and sterile smells that went with this place. I went there as often as time would allow. When someone spoke to me, I would come to the world without so much as blink. While I was there, this surrealistic world blend itself into the sterile surroundings with a smooth folding that would go seemingly unnoticed by the rest of the world. The one time that it did not come was like one of the days that were left back in memory. I was put in a diaper. This was not a happy time for me. I never in my memories ever wore a diaper. I did not care for these ladies in white. They were always so much superior to you. I didn't feel like a patient, I felt like an inmate. This last characterization I would not afford an equivalent to until I started working in a correctional facility in 1987. It wasn't as sterile, it wasn't as lonely, but it was segregated. The difference was that I had my window to the dairy and my world built on the counterpane of my bed. I remember first reading the poem, "The Land of Counterpane", and felt it like it was a window to the magic world that attended me in that hospital.

But there were times… times that I could not go to that world of warmth and comfort. The boy in the next bed would receive treatment for his burns. This little boy would lie quietly and wait for it to begin, so would I. The ladies in white and a man in a long white coat would come into the room and position themselves around this boys bed. There would be a trolley like the one with the containers of the many coloured awful tasting objects would come on. This was not laden with foul tasting things. Instead it bore implements that would make the boy scream during their application. I would never say anything about this, but I grew to have a natural distrust of anyone dressed in white. After it was over and everyone had withdrawn, the young boy would climb down from his bed and come to play with the toys in my crib. I would let no one touch these things or disturb my land of counterpane except him. I could not even limit what he would play with. Anything that he wanted was just fine with me. I have never seen this boy since, but I remember him as though it was yesterday. That was over 50 years ago. To this day I wonder if it was his trial that triggered and held my cognizance. I remember the dark hair, the deep eyes that seemed to hold the knowledge of horror. Most of all I remember his smile as he would retreat to his bed with the treasure that he had just borrowed from my fictitious realm. Even to this day it pleases me to think that I gave him just a little peace. At the time, he didn't seem to have much of that.

THE FRINGES

It seems to me to be millennia away, but at the same time it is ingrained in my blood to the depth of my very DNA. To a person that has no understanding to what the fringes are or has taken the time to read the cursory definition in the introduction, then I will try to put it into a context that will give it life.

The day started like every other day in history or before for that matter. The special part of today was that it was Saturday. It was a day of rest for every one that is except a precious few that were on a mission. On the edge of town, in the back yard of one of the constituents, there was a small band busy in what seemed to be an endeavour that would justify its industry. The band was a group of young boys busily pounding nails into boards and parts of a playhouse that was erected in their back yard. As happens with so many people of this age, the work was becoming more work like and less play like to start causing a loss of interest in the plan at hand.

"Why are we doing this?" Was an inquiry from one young fellow.

"Just in case." Was the uncommitted answer.

"In case of what?" Persistence now.

"Well…In case we are attacked by savage Indians or something."

Now to a group of children that were located somewhere in New York City or in any major centre that didn't share this ethnic group, there might have been some media influence that might justify this, but with this group, every person of it was in some degree or other related to the example. The ethnicity of our group ranged from very light to very dark. Most of us were a varying degree of mixture from one end of the spectrum to the other.

"No… I don't think so," I said. I just couldn't picture Grandpa in war paint and feathers.

"Well shit… I don't know! What if… what if… what if the crazy old hooker over there attacks us, what then, eh?" He gazed triumphantly at the doubt on our faces as our gazes moved across the small field to where SHE lived in a smallish clapboard house on the edge of the forest fence. Well, now this was a horse of a different colour. With this new threat, we once again bent to the job at hand with renewed fervour. Of coarse, as everything, this job too came to an end. We all stood back and eyed our fortress with a critical air. Our detail to security was complete. There were nails bent over to act as a locking device, there was an old hasp that was discarded for lord only knows what reason, and there was an old lock that didn't need a key anymore to open it. We all scurried inside the fortress and took up our posts as earlier planned. Now, all we had to do was wait. And wait. And wait some more. It finally dawned on us that SHE wasn't coming. The only one that was enjoying this was the youngest in the group as he sat in a corner with his hands over his eye's giggling and saying, "Is she here yet?" over and over again. This made the author of this escapade just a tad angry.

He was an easy individual to follow, as he seemed to know a lot more than any 1st or 2nd grader than we knew. He could even get the nun's to allow him out of school early. I remember the first day of school when we first seen what the inside of a school looked like. Everyone was awestruck, except him. He sat in the desk in front of me and to this day I think that this fact alone has caused a colouring of my life if not only my early scholastic career. He turned to me and said, "Would you like to see the old nun piss herself?"

"No! No I wouldn't. And neither would you. Now just turn around and wait for Sister to come back."

He continued to smile and redirected his attention to the front of the room. He then slid from his seat and dashed madly to the front of the room. With utter abandon he scooped up a piece of chalk and began to scribble fiercely on the black board. As I watched the scene unfold, I began to recognize the artwork unfolding to a pair of anatomically correct stick men of both genders. As he completed this masterpiece, he unceremoniously tossed down the chalk and tore headlong back to his seat. While waiting for the sister to return, he sat with the most pleasant smile that I had seen him wear. When Sister So and So returned, she looked at the board and without so much as a sideways glance, she said, "Johnny, first you erase these things… then you can go explain to Father Principal just what it was you thought you were doing." He then turned to me and said, "See you tomorrow morning." I didn't see him till the following day. When I did he told me that he had just gone home. "Why did I have to bother with that?"

"Because he's the principal, you jerk!" I shot at him. He looked at me as though I had just landed from some other planet.

"So What? What does that mean to me?"

I really didn't have an answer for him at that time, and as a matter of fact, I'm not too sure I do now. That was the last I heard of it. He wasn't struck by lightning, a wrathful angel didn't purge him, I didn't see him break out in boils or anything out of the Old Testament, and so I think that he got away with it.

This was just a slight character sketch of this young man. He had a knack for getting into trouble of this kind and everyone associated with the caper gets their butt kicked and he comes out smelling like a rose.

This occasion seemed to me to be starting up like any of the rest. He stood up and said, "Alright, everyone outside." We all jumped up and fairly ran to the outside of our fortress. He then stood in front of us and yelled, "Ok, everyone tell her she's a whore!" I, at this point didn't really see the need of this. We all knew She was. She knew she was. I really didn't see the need to tell the world. They all probably knew anyway. The small fellow who was giggling said, "Why? Doesn't she know yet?"

"Just yell," he repeated. So we all started yelling and calling all the bad names we knew. After we had ran our energy down to the hoarse point, we all were rewarded with a crow cawing out its protest at our racket. We stood there, discouraged.

At that point Johnny ran into his house shouting, "I'll be right back. Don't move!!!" Don't move. Just what did he think was going to happen if we did. The little giggler did just that. He flapped his arms, stuck out his tongue, and danced in circles making rude noises with his lips. We all had to smile at this. He was the youngest in our group and the rest of us always felt that we had to kind of look after him. Not that he was any trouble; we all just felt that we should look out for him. He wasn't old enough for school yet and he was very easy to like. He always had hair down to his shoulders and this was in the 50's yet. Hippies weren't introduced to the world at that time, but it never seemed out of place on him. His hair was black as a ravens' wing and just as shinny. It would have been a crime to cut it anyway.

Just a moment later, Johnny emerged from the house. Under his arm was a Grebe shoebox, and on his face was a look of triumph. As he came down the steps of his house, he looked at our expectant faces with that silly smile that we were all getting to know so well. Just what the hell was he up to now? He walked into our fortress and with all the ceremony that his small heathen heart could muster, laid his latest scheme on the small table inside. Without a word we all waited for Johnny to open the box. Without further ado, he slid off the top and exposed to us a thing of such rapturous beauty that all of our jaws went slack in sheer wonder and admiration. There it was, the Super Deluxe Whammo catapult slingshot.

"My brother ordered it out of the back of a Superman comic," Was his only comment. We all knew that if a weapon of this magnitude ever fell to unfriendly world powers, it could very well spell the end of the free world as we all know it. Thank god that Superman was only sold in the free world.

With a reverence that was due to the afore mentioned item, he lifted from its place of rest. What a beauty! Surgical rubber, stainless steel, and a patent leather pouch that was custom made for the ball bearings that were in the matching patent leather bag that was for a source of ammunition. Without much more ceremony, he removed several ball bearings from the bag and walked out to the back of our fort. With ease born of practice he loaded the pouch, took aim, and let fly. All hearts stood still as the projectile neared its mark. From our positions, we all heard the resounding plink on her front door. 'Plink?' What the hell was that? 'Plink!' As we all looked at each other in wonder, we were rewarded with the door opening and a mass of tousled, dark, curly hair with a disgruntled face underneath stuck itself out the door with a look from side to side as to discover the source of the irritation. It was as quickly withdrawn when no one turned up. Everyone sagged in disappointment as the door closed.

"Well, hot shot?" I shot at him as the echo faded. "What now?"

"Where are the kids from there right now?" he asked thoughtfully.

"I seen them both go to the show with their aunty. Which is where I should be right now instead of here," Another kid added with a shot. Not seeming to pay any attention to the baiting, Johnny reloaded, stepped forward and fired. What happened after that has been burned into my mind with a clarity that still haunts me to this day. With a deafening crash, the large window in the front of the house shattered and crashed inwards. We all stood there stunned in the silent seconds that prevailed just following. What happened next none of us prepared for. The door flew open and this terrifying creature came hurtling out as if shot by a gun. For a few terrible seconds we all stood riveted there as our immature minds tried to comprehend what was coming across this small field at us. What we perceived was a mass of dark curly hair atop a mask of immeasurable fury, enshrouded in a purple bathrobe, and shod with large furry green slippers. As this monstrosity came at us with leaps and bounds, leaping through the tall grass to make better headway with her arms thrown out to the sides as if to sweep us all up in her horrific grasp, seemed to electrify the self preservation instinct in all of us. I turned one way to watch the cause of this dilemma in full flight up the stairs of his house. The Deluxe Whammo catapult slingshot with its precious ammunition lay abandoned in the dust. With a quick look around, I noticed that I was the only one that was left standing there to defend our fort. Without much thought to the situation, I decided my staying wasn't necessary. I too joined in the headlong flight of admitted defeat. My short legs carried me unerringly to my back door and dove headlong behind my fathers' favorite chair in our living room. I peered out from the relative safety of my fathers' chair and out of the window that exposed the front street.

"Davie?"

Oh god no, my mother.

"Davie, is that you?"

" Uh… yah Mom."

"What are you doing back there?" She asked.

Just at that moment as in answer to a call, the angry hooker was striding down the street still screaming obscenities at the top of her voice.

Seizing an opportunity to somehow escape the total truth and in the end the punishment that was sure to follow, I said, "Yah, and when I seen her coming I was scared and ran home right away." My Mother gave me one of those looks that mothers all over the world know when they want to see if your lying or not. She glanced away back out the direction that the inflamed woman had gone.

"I guess I'd be afraid too, especially if I did something to upset her."

Oh My God! She knew! How'd she do that anyway? Just as I was about to blurt out a confession, she said, "Well it's time for lunch now anyway. By the time you wash up and eat she should be gone home again."

As I chewed slowly through my bologna sandwich, I started to think of the morning and the long-term ramifications that that mornings events would bring.

I had finished lunch and as much as to my mothers' prophecy, the enraged woman had returned to her home. I was sitting in our back yard contemplating the events of the morning when the three children that lived there were on their way home with their aunt. As they past down the back lane of this street, they all waved with radiant smiles on their faces, appearing very much like children that had just had an outing and not a thing to worry about in the world. Boy, would that change when they arrived at home. As the scene unfolded to my yet immature minds eye, I pictured these children walking in on the scene that our mornings' endeavours had left for them. With a sinking feeling of guilt and remorse, I pictured myself in such a scene in my own living room. My mother cleaning up the shattered glass as we looked on with our sense of security shattered and the impotent rage we would feel at the unprovoked invasion of our home.

This was a vision that haunted me through the day and even now will conger up a feeling of remorse. How would I ever set it right? Well, I could try... but not today. I think I'd better let their mom cool down just a bit before I showed my face in that circle.

LIFE IN THE FRINGES

While living in the fringes, there is usually a variation from what would be termed normal in your world as opposed to what would be termed normal in the regular world. An example of this would be the day-to-day amenities that the world in general took for granted in the latter part of the 1950's. There are the standard things that were quite pervasive then such as water and sewer, electricity, central heating, and at that time television had just made itself known as the primary media source for the modern era. The fringes people, on the other hand, looked at these things as something out of 'Buck Rogers' which was something that we would get in the Sunday 'funny papers' back then. We knew that other people in our town had them, but the closest we would ever get to the working models were the comics in the papers. Although electricity was the one amenity that most of us could usually take for granted, we learned that while dwelling in the fringes, it was not always accessible.

While T.V. was always associated with Buck Rogers, we did have other placements for the lack of amenities. In place of central heat, we had a large wood/coal heater in the center of our living room. We did have electricity, sometimes, that was associated with one electrical outlet for the entire house. Our water was brought by truck and delivered to the 45 gal. barrel that was close to the back door of the house to save the man that delivered it tracking through your house with a 2" hose. The sewer on the other hand, was not as easily dealt with. Although it could be as colourful, it wasn't quite as simple. All along the back allies of our community there was the presence of that small, uniquely constructed building that could only be for the singular purpose that it was intended for. The outhouse. There were a few more colourful names coined in its honour, but outhouse was the most common and probably, the most appropriate. The method of handling (for the lack of a better term) the sewage disposal was a gaily-painted tanker that we called the 'Honey Wagon' that was pulled by a team of horses that would draw it up one ally and down another. This would always happen on a weekend, which for some unearthly reason or another attract a cloud of neighbourhood children that would drag along behind it on the slippery snow in winter or in the dust of summer. What the attraction was escapes me to this day. The reason that this memory is so prevalent, is what this hoard of children meant to our outhouse.

You see, when one saw the construction of our outhouse, one would have to take careful consideration of how my father thinks. My father being brought up primarily during the depression always carried the motto, "Never throw away or leave behind something today that you may have a use for tomorrow". In short, my Dad's a packrat. This is not said without some justification. Just for an example that will not take us too far off the track of the story, he bought a door with a diamond shaped window in it the year before I started school. I finally saw this door mounted in a frame in my fathers' house somewhere around my 42nd year. It wasn't there when I was 39. As you can see, my analogy of this was rather conservative.

Now, back to the story at hand. My father, now that you understand him, decided that he was going to build a structure that for all intent and purpose could be moved at the will of a single individual. What he did was to build the seat and floor on site and construct the rest of this at his place of work. It was made along the same lines as modern prefab houses. A frame covered by a sheet of light plywood formed the three walls and the only variation in the fourth wall was a place for the door. We were all thankful for this door due to the fact that either my fathers' design abilities fell away at the roof or it was just forgotten and never really completed. As it continued through the life of this structure, it never had a roof. Another design flaw in our way of seeing things came to the method of fastening the walls together. This was done with 'hooks and eyes'. The same type of fastening unit that would be used to keep your screen door closed to keep flies out during the summer months that were infested by them. These devices worked well at this intended use, but fell short of perfect when the mob of children following the 'Honey Wagon' descended upon our outhouse. It was nothing for a kid with a hockey stick to run inside our outhouse and dislodge the hooks from their eyes. Once done we would come out of our house and there would be the walls of our outhouse laying flat on the ground with the last issue of the catalogue flapping in the breeze telling everyone what our lot was if we ran out of toilet paper before payday. This was the disadvantage of having the only prefab outhouse in the neighbourhood; there was an entirely different dilemma that followed not having a roof.

Behind us, along our back ally, lived a kid we used to call "ka-poh". He had developed an almost compulsive obsession with our outhouse to a point where it could have left him permanently damaged if there was no psychiatric intervention at some point or another. The inventiveness of this young man was something of a marvel (or so we thought) at his age and stage of development. There were at times a number of horrible things that were hurled over the walls of our outhouse from time to time. The fact that we could not catch him, coupled with his unerring ability to divine whether or not someone was using the facility, lent use to believe that he had not only found an extremely good hiding place, but the ability to attain it before capture.

Some of the things that were thrown over these ramparts were rocks, snowballs, chunks of fire wood, and worst of all…cats! There is absolutely nothing that could be more disconcerting while attending to one of natures most natural and private calls than to have to attend with a pissed off feline that has just suffered the abuse of being hurled through the air, over a wall, and into the presence of a half-dressed human. Its first impulse is to wreak havoc on whatever living creature that it can apply claw to at that time. If it happened to be you taking time out at what should be a quiet and private endeavour, it could cause a person physical and probable psychological damage. It would definitely raise anyone's anxiety levels about toileting. I wonder what Freud would have to say about this? It might even open a new field of research. "Anal anxiety developed in post toilet training experiences". Well, sounds about right to me. Anyway, this situation lends itself to a tale that is best told in anonymity as well as with the humour it deserves.

It was as I remember the first significant snowfall of the winter. As with all the neighbourhood children, I was outside involved in the building of snow forts, engaging in snow ball fights, and most importantly, avoiding the company that had come to visit our house in the form of young teenage girls. Now, there is nothing that I as a young boy of just barely school age that I could tolerate less than teenage girls. There was one that particularly picked at my tolerance to an extent that I could honestly say that she drove me crazy. It was not so much that she bothered me in particular, but just her overall affect drove me to distraction. She would giggle, titter, flounce, wave her ponytail with what seemed to be deliberate jerks and spasms of her head, and play with her cats eye glasses as if they were mounted on her face with the sole intention of giving her ditsy hand waving purpose. This one I would go to any lengths to avoid. So, luckily it was a good day to remain outside. Having tired of the snowball fights and castle building, but not yet ready to go inside and experience aggravation, I was sitting in the back of our coal shed engaged in God only knows what game that would occupy on a solitary basis, when the back door to the house came open and out flounced the cats eyed glasses. Her flounce was even easier to notice due to the fact that she was wearing a new pair of stretch pants that clung to her ample bottom like a second skin. Under her coat was the all to familiar bulge of the roll of toilet paper that heralded her intention of using the outhouse. Without really knowing why, I crouched down to where I could not be seen, but still watch. As the teenager disappeared into the outhouse, I saw a movement around the back of ka-pohs house. There he came. With him he carried a large slush ball about the same size as a large dogs head. I sat in stunned silence as the scene unfolded. He reached the back of the outhouse just as the unmistakable sound of trickling water started. With both hands on the slush ball, you could see him as if he was counting to three and then he threw the missile straight up in the air with a practiced ease. Just as the missile reached the apex of it's trajectory, the back door of ka-pohs house was slamming behind him. "Whoa!! Was he fast or what," I thought in amazed admiration. I turned my attention back to the outhouse just as the missile disappeared inside. There was a resounding "whoomp" followed by a moment of stunned silence. There then came a keening wail that shattered the silence and brought me bolt upright from my place of hiding, as the author of the noise came shooting out of the door in a headlong dash to the house. Hair soaked in dirty snow, cat eye glasses hanging from one ear, in one hand she brandished the roll of toilet paper and in the other the waistband to her stretch pants. In her headlong flight to the house, one leg of her pants that had come down over her toe had snagged onto something just under the snow sending her sprawling and sliding along the packed path. She stood up, fastened her pants, and still making the high pitched wail, set off for the house with the glasses still suspended from one ear.

I followed the whole scene with total abandoned amazement. As I looked over the scene, my eyes came into contact with that of the urchin from across the ally as he peered out of his bedroom window. Our eyes locked just for a second and he smiled a small smile as he sank out of sight into the backdrop of his house. For that second, there was an unspoken camaraderie that gave my assurance of secrecy. This is a secret that I have kept to this day, only revealing my knowledge of this happening in this text.

The rest of my day was rather anti climatic after this event, but the incidences with our roofless outhouse continued until the coming of the water and sewer. With it went the Honey Wagon and other not worthy things, which really signalled that change was coming to our community.

MORE FRINGE LIFE

There are times in all children's lives when an adult will insinuate some good, (or so they suppose,) idea into a kid's life. I was in the back ally, taking advantage of the previous nights rain that made huge puddles in the plentiful potholes of the ally with the neighbourhood nemesis, the Ka-poh. Ever since the snowball incident, we've had a pretty good friendship going the Ka-poh and me. On this particular day, we were trying to drain all of our pothole mud puddles into one and were busy building dikes and canals to accomplish this task. As it was still fairly early, we went about our play with little or no interruption. As we were planning the next step in our project, the call came.

"Daaa..Viiiiid!" It was my mom's voice. I was going to keep on as if I hadn't heard, but I knew that would be impossible.

"Hey, your moms calling you", the Ka-poh stated the obvious.

"Ya, I know. Look I'll be right back. Don't flood Holland yet", I yelled over my shoulder as I raced for my back yard.

"Hurry up, if you take too long the water will dry up before you get back", Ka-poh yelled back at me. I hurried into the house to ask my mom what was so all fired important as to interrupt the construction of canals to set Holland awash.

"It's lunch time", she answered to my unasked question. "And after lunch you will go with Mrs. Popkoff. She's taking her oldest and the Cordites oldest to the high school gym this afternoon". The way I looked on it, lunch was ok, even welcome, but why would I want to spend an afternoon with girls, especially those girls. They were the whiniest and about the most female girls that lived in the neighbourhood. Don't get me wrong, that was ok, but when they played it always resembled some sort of game with dolls and house and the like. They didn't climb trees or they didn't build forts or any such stuff. To them a mud puddle was something that probably belonged on another planet. Preferably one they did not live on.

"Why?" I asked simply.

"To learn to twirl a baton", came the simple reply. Now, if my mom would have told me that our dog had died, or someone in the family had been diagnosed with an incurable disease, or if I was going to attend summer school, I would have been more prepared than

I was for this calamitous news. My mom hated me. She must hate me. If she made me do this, she must know that I must die in order to escape the hell that would come after. I mean death would be the only escape from the certainty of being ostracized by my peers. I sat in stunned silence, my mouth hanging open exposing the chewed bite of bologna sandwich in my mouth as the rest hung limply from my immobilized hand. My mind was blank. The only thing to do was the old standby.

"Eh, Mom, I stammered out, "as much as I'd like to... I can't go", I tried to say, "I'm sick."

"Really," my mother had a way of telling you she wasn't buying it with out coming right out and telling you that you were lying, you would actually tell her yourself. "Just what seems to be the trouble Davie?"

"Uh... Black plague, yah, that's it I heard its going 'round this year." I squeezed my eyes shut and cursed myself inwardly the second after I had blurted out the nature of my dilemma.

"Really? Well, to my understanding the best cure for that problem is to get out and about and get fresh air and exercise." All this said with out taking her attention away from the task that she was doing at the time.

"But Mom... if the other kids see me I'll be teased until I'm 50," I blurted out with soul felt trepidation.

" 50… No, maybe 40 or so, but I hardly think 50," she said with a scarcely disguised lilt of sarcasm.

"But Mom…!" I couldn't finish as my desperation turned to despair it seems I could see myself in my overactive Childs imagination "Bearing the slings and arrows of outrageous fortune" as my life disintegrated before my very minds eye. Why didn't God intervene in these very trying times? Why didn't he send an avenging angel down to whisk my mother off to heaven where every one wants to go anyway and I know she would be happier there and I would not have to attend baton practice? I tried to assuage my guilty feelings by pretending that I was thinking of her good. Oh shit! God knew better anyway. He wasn't about to take my mom just to keep me out of baton practice. In truth, the only option for me was to go and hope that no one would get wind of it. How's that for wishful thinking?

Well, the time came that we had to be off to whatever destiny would weave for a social outcast at six years of age. It must be the same with any condemned man, as you near the place of execution, one looks for the faint hope of rescue. So rather than dwelling on any of the horrors that were coming, I busied myself with watching for the cavalry or some other rescuing body to come to my defence. Well, none came. So here I was standing at the entrance to the high school auditorium. One last glance to see if anyone will come to the aid of a desperate kid. Nope! So, now the moment of truth.

As we walked in out of the midday glare of the sun and into the din of the auditorium, I was struck by the presents of so many girls. I knew in my mind there had to be this many female persons in our small town, but who in their right mind would want to collect them all under one roof much less all in the same room. As my eyes accustomed themselves to the light in the room, they also searched the present adults for the author of this madness. Finally, my attention was captured by a man with a baton in his right hand, his left hand placed with purpose on the left hip, as the knee came up his right hand would lift the baton on high and when the knee was at the apex of its trajectory, the toe of his shoe would be pointing at the ground as if indicating to the public at large where the intended place of contact would be next. As the leg came down, the baton hand was drawn across the body to the opposite hip. As my attention came to the face of this person, I was struck by the visage of ecstatic euphoria stuck mask like on his face. All of this to the tune of a marching band blaring away on the little monograph record player on the stage in the front of the room. Stumbling behind him came a trail of small female children, mimicking the action to the best of their small child ability. Back and forth from one side of the room to the other, he would traipse this string of ducklings to the tinny blaring of the little record player. I was dumbstruck to say the least. The mans face was tilted slightly sky ward as if looking for an angelic presence in the auditorium. I knew none was there. If anything I expected men in white coats and a butterfly net to swoop in and carry him back to the asylum from whence he came.

At this point I rolled my eyes to heaven with a silent prayer of delivery. These people are mad! They can't really expect me to do this wild thing in the trail of this mad man or do they? A quick look around to the adults standing and watching and there it was, that broad beaming mother smile that is given to all children when their mothers think that they are doing something cute. "Oh God, Help Me!!" My mental cry when out to this most powerful of celestial beings. This was not just a silent prayer anymore, but a fervent plea. The panic was now starting to form in my breast as the escapee from the asylum started to wave the other latecomers to join them. I was desperate. Desperate times called for desperate measures. As this refugee from a sanatorium approached our little group, I started to conjure up the most disgusting thoughts of dead rotted gofers, rotting skunks, and whatever else my fertile little mind could conjure up in a moments notice. It worked. My very touchy stomach rolled over and I projectile vomited orange freshly stained, chewed bologna sandwich all over the auditorium floor. With not so much as a by your leave, I turned to the adult that I came with and said, "Gee, I guess I don't feel so good. I guess I should go home". I turned and started towards the exit. Before I took two steps, a hand descended on my shoulder and as I turned to find the person attached to the end of the arm, a sense of dread came over me as I came face to face with the mad man.

"Well now, I think our young man here is just a tad nervous. I think in time he may settle down and feel better later to join us, hmmmm?" He said with that same effervescent smile plastered on his face. As I stared in to he face of this mad man, I could not escape the feeling that I was about to be whisked away to some baton twirling hell from which there was no return or salvation. Faced with this new terror, I did as any other child faced with this calamitous situation would do. I closed my eyes, tilted back my head, opened my mouth, and let go with the worst full-throated howl of fear and dismay my little body could produce. I had no real idea of the full potential of this god given instrument, but I was about to learn that it was quite significant. While the echo was still reverberating from the metal in the rafters, I opened my eyes to observe what effect my new strategy had wrought. With a feeling of satisfaction, I seen that all eyes in the gym where fixed unerringly on me. When I glanced at the man with the smile from hell, he was still smiling where everyone else was staring in wide unfettered amazement. A shaft of fear clutched my heart as he looked over at one of the parents who were staring in slack-jawed awe, and said, "What a wonderful voice! All will hear it across a huge parade square"! My heart sank. That was it. I had no other tricks up my sleeve. For the first time in my short existence, I wished that Johnny were here. He would have pulled something off to even to discourage the effervescent smile. But as luck would have it, I was on my own.

At this time in my life I had very few examples as to what tough times were, but at this moment I was at the extreme edge of where I thought that the depressions of life could take me. To say the least, I was mortified! What lot was mine with my peers and contemporaries? A social outcast… to say the least or a pariah… for sure. What slings and arrows would I be subjected to now was only for me to guess. With this weight slung fully on my immature shoulders, I trudged forward to accept my fate and dance the dance of death with the other ugly ducklings stringing behind this questionable personage leading us around the gymnasium amidst the tinny blaring of the marching music emanating from the stage.

What lot was mine? I learned to twirl a baton. This was an acquired skill that I would never admit to until much later in my life. As a matter of fact, I am at this moment considering a pen name as a signature for this story, but...maybe not. Oh what the hell, it still makes for good storytelling. This did end in secrecy, but now is the time for its' telling.

CHOP-CHOP

There are some things of the past that haunts like an old wound that has never quite healed properly. One will look back and see all the things that were never set right in your past. The memory is slowly replaced by a hollow ach that slowly melds itself to the present feelings so that although it is unnoticeable, all it needs is a nudge from the pre-conscious to pull it back to light with all the intensity of a new cut that goes to the very marrow of our spirit. Soul deep is this pain. The knowledge of a loved one lost and forsaken with no ability to set the sands of time to right and no ability to ask for forgiveness even though it would surely be given. The very soul of forgiveness, loyalty and protection was our friend Chop-Chop. Of all the souls that I have encountered in my travels through this lifetime, his was the most... human.

My relationship with this animal was an exceptional one. To most people around us he was just an exceptional dog. To me he was protector, friend, companion, and the one who set most of my mistakes at that time in my life to right. If I decided to hang with the mischief-makers, Chop-Chop would cut me from the madding crowd and see me safely out of the mess. If I were ever threatened, it would be he that was between the danger and myself. If he felt that any of us were being mistreated, the tormenter would surely face his wrath.

The time comes to mind when a couple of the young guys my father worked with were being what young men are, pains in the ass. The difference was my mother was object of their adolescent provocation. She was hanging out cloths on the clothesline at the back of our house. Jimmy and Kenny were in the ally throwing snowballs at her while she tried to finish the wash. Although she was in no real danger it must have aggravated her somewhat as she voiced her disapproval with an air of tolerance. Chop-Chop, who was lying asleep on his doghouse, got up, stretched, and as if he were uninterested ambled over to where the two young men were throwing snowballs. As he drew level with the two men, he was about a foot away from the lead fellows knee. Jimmy looked down at the usually complacent animal just in time for Chop-Chop to reveal a formidable set of teeth, eyes blazed with a very undesirable light, and a growl that seemed to come somewhere in the earth under the dog. Although there were no words, the message was crystal clear and it said, "She doesn't like that, I don't like that, and you will stop it now!"

Jimmy froze and although the message was non-verbal, he understood with certain clarity. "Uh… Ken, I think we shouldn't throw any more." As he said this, his hands crept slowly into his groin as if pre-warned of the level of attack about to ensue. With his hands firmly clutching the area he felt most exposed.

"Hey Jim, if I throw another snowball, you could get the position of lead soprano in Father Principals choir. Ya' think?" Ken shot back at his friend. As he looked at the dog, the expression changed from one of joviality to a look of genuine concern. Not for Jim, but for himself as the dog was now looking at him, as he was the last holding a snowball. When the snowball hit the ground at Kenny's feet, the animals' demeanour once again changed to one of passivity and true indifference. Chop-Chop headed back to the peace of his house acting as if the two men had vanished into air. Only once did he look back to see if the two were following his directive. One stood still clutching his groin, and the other hand still outstretched as though he had just released the snowball. Satisfied, the dog jumped to the top of his house, once more laid his head on his paws, and with a last glance in their direction, closed his eyes and continued his nap that was interrupted by the snowballs. Thus, Chop Chop watched over the members of our family.

His family.

There were times that there was more on our plate than could actually be appreciated by this dog. At least that is what one would reason using the fact that the dog is non-verbal so one would think that he could not fully appreciate the depth of the ramifications that the activity would bring about. We knew better. Truth is that he would sacrifice his safety and in actuality his very life to assure our safety. The proof of this is in the action that the dog would take when anyone was threatened.

When I was in grade one, Chop-Chop would take me to school and see me home after it was over. We knew that he would follow me, as I was the youngest and most vulnerable. The older boys would always have some activity after school any way and he wasn't one to be kept waiting for those he felt could look after themselves. He would meet me at the gate of the school with his partner, a small mongrel that was a cross between a Russian wolfhound and a cocker spaniel. What a mix. This idiot animal was just as stupid as Chop-Chop was smart. If one truly knew how smart this dog was, the IQ's of the dogs were direct reciprocals. If Chop-Chop was a genius, Charley was a moron. My father would carry on conversations in French with the bigger dog as if he were bi-lingual. If one would watch the conversation for any length of time, it would be easy to concede the fact. One day I asked my father about this and his answer to me was, "Of coarse he understands. All dogs speak French, and all wild animals speak the native tongues of their areas".

How many times had this dog come to my aid, I could not dare to count. One time that comes to mind was when a dog team from down the lane had gotten loose and I was in front of them when they emerged into the ally. No one knows how this happened and I didn't care at the time. They were scary and lead by the lead dog that did not seem to like me very well. He walked up to me, stuck his nose in my face and showed his teeth. That was as far as he got. Chop-Chop tore into him and had him on the ground before I could blink. The rest of the team, 5 dogs in all, joined in the melee'. Chop-Chop ran into the deep snow of a small field and continued to fight the dogs. I ran and picked up a broken hockey stick to use as a club and ran back to help my dog. As I watched the scene unfold I saw that he needed no help from me. In the deep snow, the dogs with shorter legs could not move as well as he. His long wolf like legs gave him a decided advantage in the snow. As he fought from drift to drift, the other dogs could only come at him one at a time. By the time the fracas was over, two of the dogs were dead and the other three had to be put down due to the seriousness of their wounds. After the fight, Chop Chop trotted over to me, sniffed to see if I was all right, and shouldered me in the direction of my fathers' house. I obeyed without question.

Afterwards, sitting on our back porch, I examined him closely to determine the extent of his injuries. There was no real need. He had a few scratches, a cut over the eye, and wet either from the snow or the dogs trying to get a hold on him. He was fine.

Another time was on my way home from school. On of the classroom bullies had decided to take an interest in me. We continued down the lane under this boy's harassment trying to ignore the stupidity that was directed towards me. The bigger boy was not used to being ignored, so he ran ahead of his entourage and pushed me from behind. At the moment this boy touched me, there appeared in the area between him and me the most formidable set of ivory found in a canine mouth. This was attached to a dog that did not seem intimidated by his bullying in any way.

"Call off your Dog", he stated with faltering bravado.

"Nope. As a matter of fact, I think I'll let him eat you. He likes to eat bullies", I said with mock severity.

"No he doesn't!" This was said with a sliding scale of conviction.

" Oh, don't worry, after he gets a good taste of you, he'll spit you out. He won't eat shit. He's a very clean dog," I said with over emphasized candour. There was still that unmistakable growl that seemed to emanate somewhere in the earth beneath the dog. The bully backed off and satisfied himself with following at a distance hurtling insults at us. It wasn't until we came to the place were my father works that he had finally built up the courage to get closer to us. Throughout the haranguing, Chop-Chop had ignored the kid with an indifference that he showed all that he had little or nothing to do with. Just then a carefully aimed rock past by me and hit Chop-Chop with a thunk! Chop-Chop started, but I didn't think that the missal really hurt him. The little bastard was grinning with the knowledge that this newfound weapon gave him.

"I think that if your dog bites me, I'll tell my Dad, and he's got a gun, and he'll shoot the stupid dog!" He chorused, with a bullish smile. As he bent down to pick up another stone, I truly saw red. His back was toward me and as he bent his backside presented an irresistible target. Without taking time to weigh the consequences, I charged straight at his behind with my arms outstretched. The moment that I made contact with him, I knew there was no turning back. I was committed to doing this bully in. What I found was, I really didn't need to do much more. He hit the mud puddle nose first and it made a mighty wake as it ploughed through it gravel bottom. As the boy came up for air with a mighty intake of breath, a howl started that began somewhere in the back of his head and exited his mouth with the piercing sound of an air raid siren. All the men who were working on the loading dock of the warehouse had seen the dastardly deed that I had committed. I knew that I was in for it, because the foreman who was working the loading dock had close association with my Dad. As a matter of fact his very words were, "I seen what you did David and I will tell your Father", as he admonished me with his finger from the distant loading dock.

On the way home I was in a quandary as what I should do. The squealing Bully had long since vanished down a lane that would take him to his house and I was heading in a round about way of coming home. I had to decide what to do. My father was the fairest man that I knew, but I also knew how he felt about dogs that might bite kids. He felt that any dog that would bite a child should be put down for the safety of all children. This was not a bad credo to adopt as he did have seven children to think of. I think that the only real mistake I made in this little fracas, was not trusting the good judgment of my father. My mind was made up. I would take the blame and allow others to draw a conclusion on what the scrap was about. That way I would not have to tell a lie and Chop-Chop would be safe. Not a bad bit of a plan. The clincher in my plan was that the only two witnesses to the fracas were mute. I have long past given up the term "dumb" when it comes to dogs. Chop-Chop was anything but.

I arrived home and was met by my mother as usual. She took one look at me and, "what's wrong David?" I wasn't much at keeping secrets either. To me it was something like lying. You had to hide something and I just was too transparent for that. I quickly blurted out the story of how I had been arguing with this bully, and how he had thrown a rock at Chop-Chop and of how I had pushed him down. In the mud hole, face first, while his back was turned. Just about then I thought that I had better just shut up. It was sounding worse as I went. All this time Chop-Chop sat with his baleful eyes fixed on me as if to say, "That's enough Dave. You don't need to get yourself in more trouble on my account." When the day was done, I had been punished befitting the level of my crime. Chop-Chop was safely sleeping atop his house as was his custom, and all in all, the thing came to rest with no one being the wiser. I let it drop, because I knew on closer evaluation my story would fall apart being built out of straw the way it was. In retrospect, I would have to say my lean towards the truth would have been cemented that day, and later I remembered the quote of Samuel Clements (Mark Twain) that went, "If I never tell a lie then I won't have to remember anything. My memory, being what it is, presses me strongly to remain in a truthful mode." My memory, being what it is, seems to hold onto detail that remain in fact. Anything concocted seems to vanish like the mist in a clear morning sun. I think I like it best this way.

We had sled dogs. Somewhere in a fit of lapsed judgment, my folks allowed my brothers and myself; I was always included by the oldest when he knew there was work to be done. I was small, even for my age, but was dependable when it came to do the work. Therefore, I would always be included when these enterprises came to fruition. We bought, out of our meagre savings, a Siberian Female, known as Gyp and an Alaskan malamute dubbed Betty. Both of these dogs had a solid heritage, but both were flawed, in their own way. Betty was too old to pull in the traces anymore and Gyp was a surviving offspring from a dubious mother called Gypsy. She, Gypsy, had a habit of killing all her pups and Gyp it seemed had taken on this unpleasant characteristic. Betty on the other hand ate, slept, and produced puppies in copious numbers. An excellent mother and was probably the mainstay of our team. It was recognized by my mother that both of these breeds had very strong characteristics that where good for the sled dog, the Malamutes legendary strength and stamina and the graceful speed of the Siberian. Both were noted for their stamina, but the trappers had Malamutes to work their trap lines and haul their wood, and the Mounties and National Post of the day preferred the lanky wolf-like speed and power of the Siberian. They could do freight, but the more powerful Malamute was the dog for this task. My mother reasoned that a cross breed of both would find an animal somewhere in between that could be good at both. With this in mind, we started forth on an enterprise to make us rich and famous, again. Remember, this was the 50's and everything and anything seemed possible.

Now in our smallish town, we were cursed with a group of people that had a tendency to run things, because the real people were to busy with the more important things in life like making a living, providing for families, taking care of their own enterprises, and general stuff like that that made life in a small northern town the vibrant thing that it was. They didn't have time to worry about who was doing what, and who was doing who, or just what was happening in the next-door neighbours back yard as you had your own to worry about. There are those, however, that have no real industry of their own so they must involve themselves with the concerns of others in order to give their nothing lives something of a purpose. Down our lane, about half a block was just that type of person. This person had become someone on the town council, probably because no one else wanted the dubious position to start with. I can't remember much about elections in those days, because the incumbent usually won through lack of interest. There was usually very little publicity to commemorate these things. Anyway, this person took an interest in our dogs. An article in the local paper came out and stated with much consternation of how we had 20 some dogs penned and chained in our back yards. It was necessary for all the people of our smallish community to ensure that nothing of this magnitude could happen in our community.

As all of our dogs were kept out in the bush that surrounded our town, as I might add were every one else's, my mother went over to our neighbour to ask where these twenty dogs had come from and just what was he talking about. This particular individual was at best a coward, as he did not even talk to my mother concerning the problem. The dogs that were in our back yard were old Betty, Gyp, Chop-Chop, and of course his idiot counterpart Charlie Brown. There was a meeting of the family and it was decided that the two huskies would be moved out to the site the other dogs had, Chop-Chop who had adopted us would be moved back to his original owner, and seeing as the idiot counterpart was our responsibility to begin with, he would stay. I was not happy to say the least. My friend was not for sale or up for barter. When I voiced my concerns, I was pooh-poohed as not having a head for business and I was too young to see the big picture. Big picture be dammed! This was a family member that we were talking about. You don't sell them down the river like that. But I was to small to hold a voice in that forum. The other dogs were valuable. They had a monetary significance to them. They must come first. For the first time in my short existence I felt defeated. Of course we didn't reckon on Chop-Chop. When we put a collar on him and took him 'home', he suffered this all as Chop-Chop usually did. With forbearance with the people he loved. They gave him to the man; the man had no sooner put Chop-Chop in the house, than he made a beeline for the door, dashed through it and the man stated without a doubt that he would not have this dog back. Another person, interested in dogs' thought that Chop-Chop would make a good lead dog. He was right, of course, but Chop-Chop had other ideas. He would slip his chain, eat his collar and escape back to where his adopted family was. I remember the last time he went away. The man that had taken him came to get him and Chop-Chop ceased to fight. As the guy was talking to my brothers, my friend looked at me and with a feeble wag of his tail and a look of sorrow in those already sorrowful eyes, told me that this was over. I went to where this dog lay and putting my hand on the trusting noble head, spoke to him as only a child and an animal of his calibre could. The communication was complete. "I'll come and see you after school on my way home. Don't worry; you'll be okay, honest. I'll bring stuff for Ya'. It won't be so bad, you'll see." A press from a cold wet nose against my cheek was the last act of interest that I seen from him. I was true to my word. I would hurry down to the place where Chop-Chop was kept and I brought him things to put around his collar and he would lay and suffer the acts as he always had. There was a time that I knew that it was over. Chop-Chop had come from Northern Dogs with much the same survival instinct that they had. Even though I was his trusted friend, the one thing that even I could not do was touch his food. If you digressed and did this the low earthy rumble that came from the dog was your only warning. As I visited my old friend, the lethargic state that he was in bothered me. Looking around I had seen that he had not eaten his portion of food that day. Without thinking, I reached over to the plywood piece that it was on and moved it over to where he was. As the food was placed in front of him, his eyes snapped up to stare directly into my own. As I started to move slowly away from the food, his nose swung listlessly down and with a tentative lick on my hand I knew in my heart it was over. He had given up. When he looked back up at me the thing that I had noticed in his eyes earlier and had not identified, was a broken heart. I wrapped my arms around the furry neck and hugged him with a feeling that I could mend this with all the outpouring love that I had for this truly noble friend. I ran my hand over his head and reassured him that I would be back another time to minister the same affection that my heart had poured out to him. I never saw my friend again. When I returned to the place some days latter, his place was empty. He had escaped! My heart sang with the thrill that he had mended and with the uncommon intelligence that was his trademark, vanished. All the way home I looked for the familiar white and black markings on all the strays that I saw to see if my friend was back. The days wore into weeks. The weeks wore into months. There was still no sign. One day I had the opportunity to see the man that last had Chop-Chop talking with my older brother and I thought I would ask him if he knew anything about Chop-Chop.

"Well," He started, as if reluctant to go on, "I just wasn't having any luck with him. He wouldn't pull, he just lay in the traces and let the other dogs pull him. When I put him with my lead dog, he almost killed my best lead. I couldn't keep him and no one else wanted him so I took him to the pound and had him put down."

I said nothing and walked away. I was stunned. Chop-Chop was gone. Really gone. As nothing seemed to help the feeling that I felt at this time, I went to the only place that I had been able to go in my life and spill my misery. I made my way to the cathedral found my way inside, knelt and said a prayer for my dog. I knew that he had to be in heaven, where else would one of such a pure heart go? So I asked God to please look after Chop-Chop and be sure no one touched his food, he didn't like that.

FRINGE DEVELOPMENT

Just what can you say about development in the fringes? First, it seems like an oxymoron in that there is no development in the fringes, unless expansion of territory counts. The problem here is that the fringes are inhabited by people and people, always look to development and the improvement of their lot no matter the circumstances from which they come. I think what I am trying to say is that you cannot call development the attainment of what others take for granted. When we moved to the country, we left behind most amenities that the regular populace takes for granted. Now, this is not what one would consider an amenity, but actual services that most in the modern era take for granted. Television seems to be a good example of a lost amenity that people take for granted. Well, we gave that up. We had to. A television needed electricity in order to operate. And that is something we did not have. A one-hour school bus ride was a bit of an inconvenience, but in this case there was a one-mile walk before catching the damned thing. It was not that these things in their selves were a bad thing, but they would compound. We didn't have electricity so in the country that meant no plumbing; we had no plumbing so that meant hauling wash water from the dugout. Now one would think that this was one way of finding a final solution to the problem, but it would always come back to the original and start all over again. We hauled wash water for things done by hand, but we had no electricity so we had to take laundry to town to the Laundromat and so on and so on.

Before we go any farther, there is something that I must interject at this point. We were poor, true. We were so poor that sometimes it would hurt financially just to pay attention, but on the other hand, we were happy. We were fed, clothed, sheltered, and didn't know how truly poverty stricken we really were. When they say that ignorance is bliss, it does have merit. We pitied people on welfare. It didn't occur to us that they had electricity, running water, flush toilets, etc., Things that we would look upon as a luxury, things that everybody had, even in the fringes. We heated with wood (it was free), we lighted our house with kerosene lamps (it was cheap), and we had an outside toilet. Now this is another story and we will get into it later. We also entertained ourselves. We read, played cards, board games (the primary Christmas present), and listened to the radio that my father kept supplied with power from batteries that were supplied from his place of work. Fringe benefits he called them. We honestly didn't know that we were poor. It actually got to the point that we would bring some of these unfortunates home with us. Now, at this point some could probably see that we were poor. It sure didn't deter them from coming. One young man that I knew came to stay with us when he was around thirteen, and he just didn't leave. We accepted him as one of the family, included him in Christmas gifts and the like, and because he was an older boy, he was given a bed to himself. In my family, this meant status. He never complained about what we didn't have, but accepted what he was given with grace and dignity. What pleased my parents most of all was that he appreciated everything he was given. Come to think of it, it pleased us also that we were able to give. He was not the only one to ever come to the door and stay. There were several. When I was younger, it was nothing to come to my parents place and find the floor littered with sleeping bodies of young ones that just needed a place in out of the cold and wet. Some were gone the next day, some stayed for years. All were welcome. What saved so many of these youngsters was simply the love of the common people for his more helpless fellow man. This love that permeated our home came from the heart of my father and was administered by the companionate wisdom of my mother. Without a doubt, I have never come across a more hospitable place in all my travels and I did travel extensively. Some might say that this is easy to say about home. These are not truly my words, but reflections of what I was told by others that were gifted the graces of my parents' home. I have heard it said someplace that "Wealth is not measured by what one has, but by how little one needs." We must have been wealthy indeed, because it seemed that we needed very little. But now back to the story at hand.

I remember when TV first came to the north. It was a momentous occasion. The skyline of our small northern town became littered with antennae of the appropriate dimension to make the proper channel come in. There was only one. Everything on this channel was a week late, even the news. So what we would read in the paper one week would be on TV exactly one week later. This was, of course, at the whim of some politician that thought that if we got up to date TV, it would come from some other province that did not have the same party in power as in our province. Now wouldn't that be a disaster. Well, anyway it didn't really affect us one way or another. We didn't have power so we didn't have TV. Friday and Saturday evenings would see us on the road walking the mile and a half to our neighbours' house to watch the TV that was a week late. The last night we walked to watch TV was the year I turned 12. It was the spring of the year, getting close to summer vacation, and I remember this particular evening because my oldest brother had just informed me that there was no such thing as Santa Clause or the Easter Bunny. I was traumatized to say the least. The next day of course brought good tidings. My father had built a Television set from old TV's that he had salvaged from some of the local businesses. My parents had gone out on a limb and purchased a little generator from the catalogue that was on sale. This was one of those things that came on sale every now and then because they were not very useful in the scheme of things and were useless for any thing else but what we intended it for. To say the least, it was cheap because it was useless. It would power our TV, but it couldn't run my mothers washing machine for more than a load at a time without having to cool down for several hours after. We were allowed 2 hours of TV on Saturday night and this was a movie that was shown every Saturday night. There was a glitch though... our generator only had a fuel capacity to last one hour. The movie ran for two hours. So, Saturday night would see us staring with rapt attention watching the movie with one of us clutching the fuel can between our knees waiting for the unmistakable change in the drone of the little motor that powered our TV set. As soon as the experienced ears of the watchers detected the first falter, we would spring into action turn of the set (which my father insisted on), turn off the motor of the generator, fill the tank, start it back up, and be back in front of the TV before missing more than station identification at the predetermined spot in the movie. We had this down to a science. My father, of course, insisted that we let the engine cool down before refilling it to stave of the likelihood of gas fires. We couldn't wait this long without missing a good portion of the movie. With this style of machine, some idiot in his wisdom put the fuel tank and refill cap right over the exhaust manifold. These small engines ran on very volatile fuel call naphtha gas. An errant burp was enough to cause an explosion (another reason these dammed things were so bloody cheap). So, as we were filling this gremlin that lived in the root cellar under our house, one would have to stand at the ready with an empty potato bag to smother the explosion of flames that would shoot up when the fuel would come in contact with the hot exhaust pipe. Many were the times we would emerge from the cellar minus an eyebrow or with shorter bangs than when we went down. Sometimes our clothing would catch fire and we would try to beat out the flames without attracting the attention of a parent. It wasn't an easy task to hide one of our younger brothers that had suddenly burst into flames. Parents have a tendency to notice things like that. But we did pull it off with out too much trauma. Several minutes later, we would be back in front of the TV watching the movie and nursing whatever injuries we picked up in relative silence. It had never occurred to us at the time that we just might burn down our house or cause a catastrophe of megalithic magnitude. All we really knew was that if we did not get that machine back on line we would miss part of the movie. How is it that we develop priorities? Are they taught or do they develop from environmental necessity? This is a conundrum that I will allow some other individual to assess. I'm not so sure that I want the answer to this right now.

It may seem that we were deprived and that this story makes us seem that we should be pitied. My intention is quite the opposite really. Someone somewhere once said that life is what you make it. What I have learned is that applies to the fringes also. We were hale, healthy, and happy. We lacked for everything or did we? It truly seemed to me that we lacked for nothing that was necessary. As it was said earlier, "True wealth is not measured by what one has, but truly measured by how little one needs." It seems we needed very little. Everything that we received above that was a treat. What other people took for granted, we would view as a present. This was not done without knowing that others took this for granted. We knew that this stuff was supposed to be commonplace. It didn't matter. We still appreciated it all beyond measure. I still recall the year my mother came to us and ask if we would prefer getting electric power or having Christmas for the younger kids. We all voted for Christmas. There was not even a discussion. It was unanimous. So, once more we had a Christmas tree without lights. My father did however let us plug in the tree during TV time. It was wonderful.

Now, fringe development did not just rest with the idea of entertainment. As we lived in the country, we saw massive potential for economic growth. Livestock seemed to be the route that we should follow to economic success. Or so one should think. The truth of the matter is that we just didn't have the means to put such an operation into affect. We had the will, physical ability, but we just didn't have the means to accomplish the task.

When we first came to the county, we decided that we would get fowl and to most people that would probably mean, chickens or turkeys and the like. There was a market for these birds. The problem was where to keep them? A few birds could be kept in small makeshift pens that didn't require much money to house them. So we got ten goslings. We could heard them down to the dugout by the road, let them swim awhile and then herd them back to the small makeshift pens. When we got these birds someone had convinced my folks that one needed to feed them a special diet for their first few weeks of life. This was ok, but there was little money for extras. The starter mash was purchased anyway. No one could ever say that we didn't take the postnatal care of our livestock seriously. So, now we were the proud owners of ten geese and several bags of starting mash especially formulated for geese.

As always, fate decided to take a hand in our economic future and raised the burden from our shoulders. We woke up one morning and went to our goose pens to find all within lay waste. Our dogs, survivors of a past enterprise, had gotten into the goose house and killed all but one of the ten birds. Now the dilemma was at hand. We had lost the major part of our flock, we had to chain the dogs up while the geese or goose now, was out, and we were stuck with enough starter mash for ten birds and we only had the one with no resources to get more. Now, my father was a rather taciturn man that didn't say much when it came to this type of family endeavour. He would do what ever it was that was expected of him and would not usually offer opinions on the subject of farming. This was one of the exceptions. When the time came to wean this bird from the starter mash to grain my father insisted that this bird would finish that mash and that's all there was to it. We had all gone without so these geese could have a good start in life and the least the survivor could do was to finish the dam stuff up and just be a little grateful for the sacrifice made for them. Well… I don't really know if the bird ever truly felt gratitude, but it still had yellow feathers well into its adult life.

One would think that this would put an end to our livestock endeavours, but no, not really. Once we had come to the conclusion that we had just selected to exotic an animal, we turned our well-defined intentions to one of more basic farm stock. Chickens!

When one tries to define the most rudiments of intellectual life forms, we often will come up with earthworms, insects, or some of the single celled members of the animal kingdom. This is in no way true. The truly most stupid animal that was ever given the capacity to draw breath has to be, without a doubt, a chicken. I do mean the two legged, egg laying, morning crowing variety.

The reason that we went into this form of livestock was simple. They were cheap. You could buy 10 of these simple things for under a dollar. I do not know if it was just the times or that a chick was just very inexpensive to produce? As they were so … inexpensive, we invested a whole $10.00.

Now this means that we were now the proud owners of 100 of the stupidest animals on this planet.

Scientifically, it is said that the smallest particle whose mass can be measured is the lepton. Its atomic weight is almost, but not quite incalculable. If it were compared to the intellect of a chicken, it would be humongous, but enough of that for now.

When we had prepared a spot for our latest arrivals, we forgot how susceptible these things are to the elements when they are that young. We could not leave them in the coop outside or they would surely die. My mothers heart being made of the softest fabric on that bolt of cloth, arranged to have the chicks penned inside at night and let out in the morning. I did not mean in the coop, but inside our house. At first the space that was occupied by the chicks was small and unobtrusive. In the weeks that followed there was not only a considerable change in the amount of space required by the birds, but also a significant difference in the level of care these birds would require to keep the house more like a house and less like a chicken pen. As these animals became larger, the less effective was the means to keep them in the pen made in the house. It was just to short. To remedy this situation, my mother would station a child close to the pen with a small broom. When a bird would jump up and later simply step up on the wall, the Childs' chore was to sweep the bird back into the pen. Naturally, as these birds got larger and more motivated, the more sweeping was required. This would keep one quite busy for the evening. They would not settle until all the lights were out and everyone was in bed. The morning would bring an awe-inspiring spectacle as the chickens were released for the day. The makeshift corral was lifted, the door was opened and the 100 plus chickens poured through the door after the fashion of a dam opening its floodgates and pouring forth a feathered flood. This would take an impressive time to allow all these birds passage to the outside.

There was finally the time that my mother felt that these critters could finally go to the place that was intended for them from the onset of this enterprise. Although this was the end of this story, it in no way ended the adventures that my family would endure in the ways of fringe development.

* * * * *

With the amount of work that was mandatory to maintain in the fringes, there was always the time that leisure time was available. What did one do for ones leisure? Well, whatever one could. As we lived a considerable distance from other children, one would have to make friends wherever one could. In my case there was the old man from across the road. His name was Gordon. He had a quite sizable garden that bordered on our property so that I could look out a window and see him at work in his quite sizable vegetable crop. I would spend hours with this very interesting old man and listened to the stories of when he would work with the local lumber company. I would sit for hours on the bank of the river where he lived and could almost picture the river boats coming up the river to collect the large "log booms" that would have been prepared over the winter and placed on the ice waiting for the inevitable thaw that would bring the boats up to collect their cargos. He would tell me tales of the huge horses that would pull impossibly sized loads of logs from the forest to the river for their eventual trip to the mill many miles down stream. I would never tire of these stories and they where very seldom repeated. Each day would bring a different story and a new experience that would set my imagination running to an ageless time when all things around me had held such industry that one could scarce imagine how this quiet setting had changed from the busy to the passive. My minds eye would bring back the days of lumber crews that worked prior to the development of the agricultural endeavours that surrounded me today. I now realize that this was necessary in order to have the development of the agriculture; the forest would have to give way. And so it did. Now I sat day in and day out with this old man who was a living relic to a by-gone era. He told me stories of rogue bears and how the safety of there networked community along this waterway would be endangered by this natural menace. These stories would have a profound effect on the ways that I would view the world and how it would motivate me into starting my own paths to adventure and understanding of the world and how it truly worked.

Through the long days that I would spend with my old friend, I developed an attachment that would last me long into adult life. When the time came that he had to leave and move to a place that he had to be cared for, I missed him greatly. No matter that there was a separation brought by his absence, I still felt that he was a fellow fringe dweller no matter where he might live. It was not until I was well into adulthood that I heard of his passing, but in my mind even then, his story of how the fringes had been a place of major industry are with me still.

RIGHT OF PASSAGE

The rest of the 50's moved away with not too much more significance than can be attributed to the 50's. As we were a nomadic family we had moved several times before we came to the place that my restless parents would put down roots and finally even to this very day, stay put. Now, this was in no way a deterrent to an inventive lad like myself. It was in some ways a wonder land that the mind of an over imaginative kid would have a fields day with. Many the hot lazy days of summer would find me with my feet and legs hanging over a stack of hay while my two favourite friends and companions in the world would snuffle their way through the grass looking for unwitting rodents that would be flushed by one then eaten by the other.

I would lay and stare up to the sky and at once be an ebon skinned warrior feathered headdress aflutter as I tramped the fabled Serengeti beneath my calloused feet. Then with very little concentration or trying standing on the fabled killing fields of ancient Japan, the Samaria, a sword in hand awaiting the time to throw my life to the winds of chance and slaughter with the word of my master, and then skipping to the steppes of Russia, the Cossack, galloping madly towards a foe that has witnessed your ferocity and knows that he awaits his impending doom, or now the heroic knight awaiting the order to charge towards the overwhelming forces mustered against your lord, knowing the day contains only the slim chance of survival as you sit astride the great war steed, standing calm with the assurance of the man with his hands on the reins will pull you through the coming calamity as he has done so many times in the past. As I lay there, kingdoms were lost, countries were made, maids were saved, the universe in its entirety was tamed and charted, and Gods were born! Not a bad way to spend an afternoon, eh?

As I lay this afternoon, my reverie was shattered by the harsh thump of a diesel motor as it laboured its way to where I was sitting on my parapet to the world. As the case tractor came closer, my perch became less like a castle and more like the stack of bales that it was. The young boy operating this machine was from the farm down the road and was a few years my senior. As he pulled up, he deftly killed the motor and let the machine coast the few remaining feet to were I was sitting.

"Whatcha' doin'?" The older boy asked more out of politeness than out of true interest.

"Nothin'. Just sittin' here. How about you?" I asked.

Now his eye's lit up with real excitement and true interest, "I was out lookin' for the Rogue bear. Neighbour shot it about four days ago and its been rootin' up a field of oats, got to roarin' aroun' in the pig barns and kilt a buncha dogs that just got born. Thought if'n I could fin' him I jus' might shootem'. You haven't seen him down here have Ya?"

One look at this young man and I knew that this was a real deal. The one thing that you could bank on was that there was little or no imagined story involved here. When one went down to visit and play for the day, the play kind of made its way from forts and cowboys to rebuilding hydraulic pumps, repairing doors, feeding stock, ploughing fields, and slowly would work its way into more work than play. It wasn't that these kids didn't want to play, they never really learned how. When most kids were learning to walk after their potty training, these kids were probably trading their diapers for coveralls and their fisher price trucks for the real thing. Don't get me wrong; these guys had better coping skills than anyone my age that I knew. When things got a little too tight for them and they wanted to get revenge for the trespasses made against them, they often employed the cat. This cat that they had really hated their father. Their father was usually the main source of concern for these young guys.

On the occasion that this happened when I first witnessed this, the boy that was more my age was chastised for some indiscretion that I couldn't fathom at this time, but learned later that it had to do with breaking a plow shear or something fairly close to this. Anyway, my buddy collected his swat upside the head and was sent away from the T.V. I followed this kid into the bedroom. As he was walking away from the living room, he reached down and picked up their cat. Once away from prying eyes, we slipped unnoticed into the bathroom. He closed the door, went in under the sink, and produced a bottle of horse liniment and wood rasp. The cat was then placed on the bathroom mat, as his tail was lifted his claws dug into the mat in anticipation of the coming event. The rasp was applied in a few chaffing sweeps and as the liniment was applied to the affected area, the poor thing lost its mind.

"Quick, open the door now!" The cat unerringly tore down the hall, into the living room, and jumped on the fathers' head. The cat had slung itself over the top of this mans head holding on to one side with his front claws, while the back legs dug into the neck and shoulders of the other side. The man reached up, peeled the enraged feline off his head and threw it into the wall. The cat hit the wall and like a rubber ball bounced right back at the supposed cause of its torment. This time it landed right on the face of the man and reached around the back of his head in a bear hug and dug its teeth into the bald spot on his head. Once more the man peeled the cat of his face, but this time with a little more desperation than last, kept hold of the scruff of the neck and unceremoniously threw it out the back door.

"Dam cats nuts," he muttered to himself on his way back to his favourite chair. So turned the wheels of justice in this household.

My attention turned back to the boy telling me the story of the rogue bear. I have heard all the stories of these creatures and how they develop some kind of fevered intelligence and would wreak havoc around the county side and even develop some kind of revenge thing that would become this maddened animals obsession to the point of supernatural deeds were done by both victim and animal. As my mind spun with all kinds of romanticized notions on just what was involved and even what wasn't, the boy finally realized that he had lost me somewhere and being the pragmatic fellow that he was, really didn't want to go there.

"Well, I gotta' go now," he said without further ado, "See ya' aroun'." He reached down to the starter switch, the diesel struggled to life, and with a release of the hand clutch he was once more down the road from whence he came. As the rumble of the tractor vanished in the distance my head was still spinning with all the possibilities of an adventure in real life unfolding right here within the temporal boundaries of my world. Wow! Now all I had to do was to go out and find this cursed fiend from hell. As I slide from the haystack, my mind flew to where I would search out this evil thing. A cave. That seemed a logical place for a demented, evil, intelligence to hole up. When my mind wandered to anything that might fit this scenario, the only model of a cave I could think of was the holes that the blanket beavers made by the river and this pretty picture didn't really fit the bill that I had in mind. As I walked and got closer to the house it came to me that it didn't matter what it was that I figured out, there was no way that I was going to get away from here to go after a bear bare handed. They sure wouldn't let me go alone with a rifle. Now, how in the hell was I going to get away from the house and smuggle the old 303 with me? Dam, things like common sense and fear sure stood in the way of a lot of really good adventures.

Before I had too much time to study on the whole thing, the answer came ready made. My younger brother came running up to me and with the excitement appropriate to the situation said, "Were going down to Nora's place. Ya commin'?" This was just what I needed in order to escape to my adventure. Now, before we go any farther, I guess I should explain a few things concerning my younger brothers. These are kids that have a relationship that makes telepathy seem like a crude form of communication. Whatever verbiage they did use, became like silly putty in their capable hands. Nails became pennies; saws became cutters, hammers were pounders, and all the animals in the forest that were in reach of their creative ingenuity were reinvented and renamed to suit whatever new purpose that they were to serve. As the animals and other things that were in reach were renamed, so were our neighbours. There was no one in the valley with that name, but to the boys, they existed.

Although a visit on a day like today might have alleviated a lot of boredom, I did have another agenda to fulfill.

"Na, I'm not going. I'll just stick around the house with Buster and Straight gut". I said ambiguously.

Now, I should at this time point out that Buster and Straight-gut where the names of my two most trusted companions, my dogs. When they were to be named by the people who were supposed to be there owners, they gave them normal names like Spike and King and so on. Later, as they came to live with us, they were appropriately renamed as to there most prevalent characteristic. With Buster it was this dogs inability to produce anything of an emotion other that total boredom. Thus, he always had a very deadpan face and reminded me greatly of the master of deadpan, Buster Keaton. That is how he got his name. Straight gut on the other hand came by his through his favourite pastime, eating. As a pup, he would stick his head in his bowl and not stop eating until it was empty. He was the only dog that I've ever seen eat and defecate at the same time. When my mother witnessed this feat, she said, "If you picked that dog up by the jaw and looked down his throat you could probably see the pucker in his poop hole. That dog must be just straight gutted". Hence, the name stuck.

Even with their particular impediments, these two were my most trusted companions and just the ones to share in my adventure.

As I came to the house, everyone was piling into the car. This car was another source of interest, as it seemed to be the only one, not just in the area or province, but also in the entirety of Western Canada. I don't know how many times I've sat in the service station office and heard some guy tell my father that he had to wait for the parts for his car from Timbuktu or some other God forsaken out of the way place. I had better geography lessons from the local parts people than I did in school. But I digress.

As the car pulled away down the highway with the resounding roar of an overpowered vacuum cleaner, I immediately started to prepare my adventure.

The old Lee-Enfield was right were it always was and after some digging I came up with the clip and ammunition. As my child's mind wrapped itself around the coming hunt I was transported to the Dark Continent to a safari in search of King Solomon's mine or some other like fable.

Now, to the casual onlooker, one would not see all that was there. One would see a young boy, two mongrel dogs and an ancient weapon of a bygone war. But to perceive from the inner eye, one could not help but see a warrior preparing for a coming battle with an omnipotent and terrible enemy. One armed with the indomitable strength of courage setting forth with a clear eye and stout heart. So on it went only once interrupted as the two fearless hunting hounds got in a disagreement over the mummified remains of a gopher. Straight gut, being the bigger of the two, won out on the mummy and carried it triumphantly before us like a battle standard. After awhile, he vanished into a near by bush and returned a short time later with his mussel all covered with dirt. Well, at least the mummy had a burial.

We set out towards the place where the oat field was thinking that this area might keep the bear somewhere in its' immediate area. We had crossed several miles of summer fallow and through a few small willow patches before coming to the oat field in question. As we were into mid summer we could see the devastation in the waist high grain. It looked like someone had gotten into the field with a machine with large tires and did power turns tearing up large portions of the area with little or no reasoning. There was no pattern, none of the patterns one would normally see with an animal in search of food.

Nonsense and irrationality seemed to be the rule. Even when I started this quest with the grandiose ideas that fancifully flit through my mind, I fully expected the natural patterns of behaviour that one usually seen with these animals. As my pre-composed perceptions began to fade, the anxiety of doubt began creeping in from my preconscious. My two companions, my puppies of childhood seemed a little more preoccupied than usual. There attention focused on a thick brush area directly ahead. As we came closer to it, I began to detect the faint odour of something gone bad. Looking closely at the area, I saw a thick cloud of insects buzzing over one area in particular. As we got closer, the smell grew stronger. Well, I figured that the animal had probably crawled away and died in the bush. At least it smelled that way. For some reason known to everyone else but myself, I jacked a shell into the chamber. As I cast a cursory glance at my puppies, they were gone. In their place someone had brought forward two things that I in no way recognized. Gone was the timorous playfulness that these two were famous for. Here were two animals with all the ivory in there mouths showing. A look in their eyes' that made me think that they were staring into the very pit of hell or that they had just exited it. Straight gut my overly hungry puppy, was now some… thing that I did not recognize and Buster my dead-pan dog was gone and in its' place was this vicious snarling beast I in no way wanted to be near let alone claim. My sensibilities numbed as I returned my gaze to the bushes. There seemed to be an eternity that stretched over that deadly space between the bush and ourselves. Then, without warning or any other design, the thing in the brush broke cover and dashed towards us. The next seconds were a second eternity measured by the visualizing every horror or nightmare that my boyish mind could remember or conjure up reared up in front of me and seemed to suspend the very essence of time. Without cognition or reasoning I felt the metal plate of the rifle thump solidly against my shoulder and as the monster turned towards Buster, I felt the finger of my right hand squeeze closed and the earth shattering report of the rifle. The whole world had gone black! I heard nothing. I smelled the spent powder of the rifle shell. I had closed my eyes. My eyes shot open to once again view my nightmarish vision. It was gone. In its place were my puppies, once again themselves. Whatever hellish spirit had then possessed them was now exorcized and vanished with the nightmare that had suspended time. In its' place there was a heap if fur that the dogs were curiously sniffing. It wasn't even that big of a bundle. I jacked another shell into the chamber and as the spent casing spun away, I realized that the heap before me was the rogue bear. With the rifle pressed hard against my shoulder I kept the rifle pointed at the pile in front of me. A quick sideways glance at the dogs seen Straight Gut laying down, tongue lolling out as if he were just getting ready for a nap and my dead-pan doggie was back. I slowly let the gun down and let it point at the ground. I crouched on my haunches with the gun across my lap wondering just what the hell to do next. What could I do? It was done. Over. The hunt was a success. Why was I shaking so badly? I guess that's what you do after a successful hunt. Bullshit! I was scared shitless. There was a coppery taste in my mouth and I didn't need anyone to tell me that it was fear. At that point in time I would have been neither surprised nor ashamed to find out I needed a change of underwear. I wiped the back of my hand across my mouth and found it came away streaked with crimson. I gently felt along my lower lip until I came to the affected area. I chuckled a little to find that I had bit my lip. The problem was I don't remember when that happened. Wait 'till I tell everyone about that. That would bring a chuckle. The hell it would! If anyone found out about this my ass would be grass and my oldest brothers foot the lawn mower! Shit, that is if there was anything left of me after my Dad finished with me. I looked down at the rifle in my hand and suddenly realized that I was a 13 year old kid sitting out in the middle of a destroyed oat field with a dead bear at my feet carrying a loaded cocked rifle waiting blow his own foot off. I carefully released the bolt and pulled the clip from the rifle. As I removed the round from the chamber and slid it back into the clip, the events of the day began to settle on me like dust settling on a road after a vehicle has passed and disturbed it. As I took a closer look at my bear, I could not help but see that it not only was a small animal, it also had a hole in its' shoulder that one could see the bone in. The area around the hole was black and festered and one could see where the blowflies had been at the wound. The poor bugger must have been in some pain. It would have pissed me off too. Gone was the evil creature of my imagination and here was just some poor dumb animal that fell victim to the ingenuity of man. Today there was no wrong righted, no evil purged, just one more of mother natures children dead because someone wished him to be. There was no rejoicing this day and Mother Nature and all her children mourned the loss of another innocent at the hands of man.

As I walked home that day with my two dogs foraging ahead, it seemed there was a new illumination to this world. I would never see it the same again. From the intricate beauty of the tiniest spiders web, to the power in the poetry of a formation of flocking geese, I could never look back in ignorance and see the way I did before. I realized what had happened was wrong. My role in it just as wrong as the person who did the shooting in the first place. I went out looking for adventure at the cost of an innocent's life. I involved my dogs whose instincts were abused that were to be used in their survival. Not to insure their lives, but to cater to my overactive imagination. These two were gifts to me. Their lives to be enjoyed and treasured not risked on stupidity. I simply do not have that right. I pondered this on the way home. Wondered how I would tell about it. As I reached home, there was no one there yet so I resolved never to do such a stupid thing again and put this story into my memoirs and tell no one of my stupidity. Now, I had to figure out how to make it up to Mother Nature. Of course, I never could.

GROWTH IN THE FRINGES

How does one monitor development and growth? Is it through the gaining of knowledge, the attainment of life experience, understanding the simpler mechanics of societal workings, or simply all the above? I have heard this word "growth" represented in many ways. To us in the fringes it had an entirely different meaning than to the others within our periphery. It meant, "knowing your place".

I do not think that in all my experience with life in the fringes did I ever see a fringe dweller whose father was a business owner, a bank manager, a social worker or any branch of the civil service for that matter. Our fathers worked for all these people, but we would never sit close to them at Mass on Sunday, or get invited to the family B-B-Qs. Actually, I think that the only interaction with them was that we actually got to sit in the same schoolrooms with their children. There was other involvement of course, but not the type that could be considered a healthy interaction. Sooner or later one would lose their innocence and find that there was a sociological difference between them and us. It wasn't when we were younger; we really didn't develop our prejudices until later, but merely reflected those of our parents. We didn't adopt these as our own until much later in life and usually it was to please our parents that we accepted the mantle that they had worn and inherited from their parents. The term,

"The sins of the father visits the sons for seven generations", comes to mind at this thought. Well, this is how I witnessed this.

As I said earlier, we were poor. The usual toys like bikes and the like were not something that came readily to us. If we wanted these items, we attained them through extra curricular industry that didn't involve family income. You worked for it yourself. It wasn't that we didn't have the means to accomplish this task; it was just that to buy 9 bicycles was just a bit beyond our ability. Our belief in this area was quite Marxist, if one couldn't have it, we all did without it.

The way we learned to make extra money or any at all for that matter was to step into the fur trade. Our Father taught us how to lay snares and avoid the need for expensive traps. This would only afford a small variety of game, but it would also give us a way to get money that was truly ours. We could always get the few nickels that it would take to get more snare wire when we would need it, but the remainder of our meagre income would burn a hole in our pockets before we could save for the bigger and better things. This was our Christmas money and for special occasions. We in actuality did quite well all things told. The small animals that we would catch and trade would see us at the local festival with enough to see some local shows or even the odd movie. Bikes were for those of non-fringes personnel or for some whose fathers worked for someone that gave a good enough wage as to afford these items. This is where this story begins. I had borrowed a friend's bike.

I used to marvel at the speed one could actually get around with riding a bike. A half hour walk would turn into a few minute ride. As I took my friends bicycle through the streets of our small town, I was pleased at the way the time and miles shrunk to an almost negligible quantity. It was exhilarating to say the least.

I was riding the bike to the eastern outskirts of the town in the direction of the town dump. When I ran out of pavement and came to the gravel road that made the highway, I figured that it was perhaps time to head on home and probably return the bike. As I was riding through unfamiliar neighbourhoods, I paid little attention as to who was in the periphery of my travels. I was guiding the bike down the road without too much concern when I felt a blinding "Whack" on the side of my face just above the jaw line. The bike went down with me on it. I went over into a smallish ditch and rolled onto a grass boulevard so I came up fairly unscathed from the fall. As I got to my feet, I felt wet on the side of my face. I ran my hand over the wet spot and looked at the crimson streak across my hand. At this point I was totally bewildered as what had happened to cause this. A glance across the street showed two boys the same age as me, looking at me and smiling like Cheshire Cats. The tallest one held a slingshot in his hand. My mystery was solved.

Still feeling a bit shaky, I examined the bike for damage. Nothing to bad. Some scrapes and scuffs and stuff. Nothing to put it out of commission. I walked over to where the boys were standing and in the loudest voice I could muster after an accident, "Why did you do that? What the hell were you thinking?"

"Prove it!" The bigger one said mockingly.

"I don't have to prove nothin'. I just asked what you thought you were doing shooting people with that thing." I said indicating the slingshot. The spot that the missile had hit was now loosing its numbness and was starting to throb. I was not usually an aggressive child, but this had my dander up just a tad.

"You can't prove that I did it. You have no witnesses. There are two against one". The sneer lost its smile but kept its contempt.

"I don't have to prove nothing," I said coolly, "I know what you did and that's all there is to it". I had had enough. My balled up fist landed smack in the middle of his sneer and as he grabbed at me, I grabbed his bloody nose and levered him to the ground. As all bullies, he folded like a house of cards. I turned to the kid with him and said, "What about you, Rick? What do you think?" Just then the door burst open and an over weight man hurled himself out the door and started in my direction with surprising speed for his size. I turned and fled. I grabbed the bike got on it and started moving just as the man caught up to me. As I picked up speed, I could feel his fingers slipping from the nylon windbreaker I had gotten from the church hamper. Something less slippery and I would have been caught. Thank God for Christian Charities.

As my lead widened, I saw a familiar car pulling out from the ally. The town police cruiser. Driving it was a corporal that knew my Dad and whom I felt confident would ensure my protection. I sped the bike in front of his car, jumped off, knocked on his window, and was rewarded by his rolling down the window and saying, "Well Hello David. Is something wrong?"

I blurted out my story just as the fat man and his equally fat wife came panting up to the car. He told his story and it didn't differ too much from what I had told the Cop. The part he left out was the part about his kid thumping me with a slingshot.

"So, there we have it then. David what do you feel that you did wrong here?"

"Pardon?" I asked truly bewildered.

"Well, let me fill you in on what it was you did. You ran away from an adult and you didn't stay to accept responsibility for your actions," he said with thoughtful reflection.

"What?!" I couldn't believe what I was hearing.

"Just explain it the way you did to me and I'm sure this responsible citizen will work out the problem that you two kids have and come up with something that would be fair." He looked as if he actually believed that. With that said he grabbed me by the arm, passed me to the waiting fat man, and said, "Don't run away from adults in the future". He climbed back into his car and I felt my hope diminish as he rounded the next corner. As he did, I felt the grip on my arm tighten and didn't let up until the mind numbing blow from his open hand landed flush on the side of my head. I never lost consciousness, but as the beating proceeded, I successfully rolled up on the road were I lay to protect myself from getting too much hurt. The woman was kicking me with sandaled feet. It's surprising how much a sandal can hurt.

After the beating and listening to the diatribe on what kind of a low life scum I was, I got to leave. I picked up the bike and not being able to ride it, walked it back to my friends place. When her father saw me come into the yard with the bike in tow, he said, "What in Gods name happened to you?" At this point I did not know who to trust so rather than invoke the wrath of an Adult that I truly trusted and respected I lied.

"I fell down with the bike and so I walked it home to make sure I didn't hurt it anymore". It was the truth with omissions.

"I really don't care about the bike, David, but you come inside so we can have a look at you and see if you need a Doctor." At this point I started to feel the guilt of my deceit. I was about to spill my guts and thought better of it. I just didn't want them to think less of me and in turn scorn me as those others adults did. As the first aid proceeded, I thought that I would just forget about it and let it go. That was over forty years ago. How am I doing so far?

THE FRINGES TO AN OUTSIDER

With all that I have been writing, one would think that I was the type of a kid that wandered life like Peppy Long stocking or the original David Copperfield. I was a different type of kid. I was even the type to be labelled a nerd and receive vain mercies from my peers and contemporaries. I learned fairly young that no one would want to bother with a 'wimp' that was unpopular and would receive little notice from the teaching staff and the only hope that you had of your age mate was that they didn't notice you too much and that way you just might be spared the slaps, cuffs, punches, and general picking on that was your lot if you did not fit the mould that was painted of the ideal youngster. Everyone states that children are so cruel. Well, I'm sorry, it wasn't the children that made it this way. It was without a doubt the parents, school authorities, teachers, law enforcers, and all other adults that subscribe to the stupidity of what the life of children is or was. They all sit around in their base stupidity and state with wide-eyed amazement that they have no idea where all the violence in school comes from. They stand in shocked amazement and tell news reporters that they have no idea what the Columbine shooting was all about. Of course they wouldn't admit that they seen the happenings around the school and were too lazy or indifferent to deal with it as they are actually required by law to do. But I do digress. Actually, when it comes to these simple lazy idiots that we entrust our children to, I not only digress, but I have a tendency to foam at the mouth when it is discussed. Now, my story and how I dealt with this. After all, at this time in my life I no longer had Chop-Chop to intervene in my battles.

As the dawn of adolescence first reared its' ugly head and we separated from a generic form of children and into Boys and Girls, I began to notice the idea of the pecking order. There were the athletic kids, the kids that were good-looking, moneyed kids whose parents socialized in upwardly motivated society, the tuff kids, and the rest of us. Now, the rest of us were the kids' that ran home after school, hid at recess, got beat up allot and generally felt the hell of childhood. This without a doubt was one of the blackest periods of my young life. At lunchtime I would sneak out of the school grounds and off to a friends place where I knew I would be accepted. This too became tiring and I started to deal with it the way everyone tells you to. I went to the authorities. I went to the teacher who sent me to the principal who sent me to a school trustee. Now, this got interesting real quick. Once the school trustee learned that it was his kid that I was reporting, he sent me back to the principal, who in turn sent me back to the teacher who sat and instructed me at length on how little everyone liked a tattle tale and tried to make me admit that I was stretching the truth somewhat or that I had in someway predicated the abuse. I stood by my story and even explained how it was more than one that was the perpetrator. This was obviously not what she wanted to hear, because she waved her hand impatiently and told me that I was unreasonable and she was not going to talk to me about it if I was not going to be reasonable. As I was dismissed from the her presence, a feeling crept over me that I had not felt before and thank god, not to many times afterwards. As I tried to label this new feeling, it took me some time to equate it to anything that I could place some form of familiarity to. I finally found that I could equate it to the feeling of how I felt when I looked into the pit under our outdoor toilet when it was too full and we had to move it. I was truly disgusted. Naturally, after the School Trustee relayed my indiscreet accounting to his kid, the kid and several of his chums beat the hell out of me. They chased me down and got me wedged into the doorway of the clinic and kicked and punched me while I covered up and hoped that they would get tired or I would pass out. What happened next made all the difference in the world to me.

"Get the hell off him you little Bastards!" came through the muffle of my coat that had been pulled around my head. I parted my arms and looked up to see Tommy the taxi driver. I felt strong hands take me by the arms and lift me to my feet.

"There were enough of the little shits. Well, you don't look any the worse for wear," he said smiling. "Why didn't you fight back?"

"Seemed no use. There were too many and I may have gotten a worse licking'," I said as I tried to get my bearings. "I'm not a good fighter anyway."

"Then learn", he said as he walked away back to his cab.

People do not fully understand the impact that their words can have on people and there is no way they can appreciate the turns they can set in a persons' life. They probably don't want the responsibility either. So I set out to do exactly what Tommy told me to do, learn, and learn I did.

The rest of this school year saw me doing several things that were not in my character to do. After school, I would run down to the smallish gym under the Catholic Rectory where a small priest taught the manly art of self-defence better known as boxing. When I think back on it, I feel that this was the first time in my life that I had ever taken anything into my own hands. It was extremely empowering. I never fought any real bouts, but I would learn to duck, weave, cover and block, and I learned at a very early age at the benefit of letting someone commit and stick him with a counter punch. This paid off when I started competing in Karate and actually got me to the silver medal placement in the heavy weight division for Western Canada. I cannot say that my earlier lessons were inspired by the same motivation as in my latter Karate career, but the principal was the same.

The boxing taught me that I didn't have to take a punch, but if I did, to use the off balance position my antagonist was in to my advantage. If the other person were sure he was going to score a hit, he would usually commit himself totally to the enterprise. One of the main lessons I learned was not to allow the hit to take its target fully, or what's known as "slipping" the punch and to roll with it lessening the impact of the blow. That way one could throw a counter punch with much more accuracy and because the person was open, with much more devastating results. I was a counter puncher. Because I was a bit small for my age, this gave me an advantage to my larger peer group. My first street fight was a bully that stood a good head higher than the rest of us. Up to this point I was used to sparring with gloves on and knew that if I wanted to hurt, I would have to put my entire body behind the punch. The results were devastating. The bigger boy never tried to hit me, but made a grab for me in order to use his size to advantage. I slipped inside and threw an uppercut and would have hit the boy in the soft lower abdomen, but because of his height, my fist landed flush on his groin. The results were electric. The boy was finished, but not before I threw two hooks to his body and a right cross to the left side of his face. The fight was over and the bully lay curled in the dust, coughing blood into the dirt. The usual jeering faces that stood around and taunted you after a beating were strangely silent. I won't go so far to say that the looks on their faces were of new born respect, but the fear that I read there would have to be enough. As the fear in my own mind started to diminish, I looked up at the group whom I barely recognized with this new look on their faces. Surprisingly, the words that came out were not placations or admonishments for mercy that was never shown, but "Who's next?" No one said a word, but they all backed a step as I started to leave. As I walked away, I felt their eyes on my back as I strained my ears for some word or catcall or some comment to diminish you to the world. None ever came. As I put more distance between the group and me, the feeling of elation was one that I never had experienced in my short life. Now I knew what I had to do in order to escape the hell that I had been subjected to all my young life. I knew that I dared not loose, for if I did, the torment that I had been subjected to would return. But this gave hope! As long as I kept winning there was no one that they could get against me to return me to the subjugation that I had endured for years. I had to learn more! I must put so much distance between these people and me that they would never again beat me down. They would never be able to cross this bridge and return me to persecution. But how would I do this? I remembered a book that a friend of ours had left at home on kung fu and karate. I had learned how to use my hands, why not learn to use my feet too? Even though I poured over this book, I had seen no application for the kicking techniques until I watched Kato from the Green Hornet on TV. With the book to show me the kick and Kato to demonstrate the dynamics, I became more than passable using my feet to fight. Between the book, the little priest, and Kato, I built myself a reputation to wrap around myself as an insulator. I was good enough to get lumped in with all the tough kids and shared their autonomy and their reputations. Of all of the kids in our school system, they made a class for a short while that all the "trouble makers" were lumped into. Teachers, principals, school board officials, and most of the "authoritarian" structure disliked us. The truth of the matter was, that they had created us through their stupidity and indifference. But this is another story. The one I tell now is how one very intelligent young woman dealt with the problem and actually reached a group of kids who were heading for the skids, so to speak. It even stopped some of us from arriving there. The ones that were not reached were already gone.

* * * *

The first day of school was just like any other day that had been the first day of school. There was one difference though, the order of the classroom. There was close to twenty of us and only one girl in the group and her nickname was 'Rocky'. She was without a doubt one of the toughest kids in our smallish town. She could scrap with the boys, play all the rough sports and no one ever gave Rocky a rough time. If they did, they always came out the worse for wear. All of the toughest kids in my peer group were in that class. I suppose that they thought that if we were all kept under one roof that they would be able to keep better track of us. The truth was that they either didn't have the guts to deal with us, were truly indifferent and thought that if they ignored us and put us away in some corner, we would vanish, or truly had no idea of what their pious little system had created so hadn't the foggiest how to deal with this conundrum. Well, you can bet that we weren't going to set their atrophied little minds at ease.

When we finally realized what had happened, there was a mix of feelings on the whole issue. At the time I wasn't sure that I liked it very much, but could not quite put my thumb on it. What I put together latter was that they didn't want their children associated with the likes of us. The way they actually saw the big picture was that 'we' were victimizing 'their' children. Even if they realized that we were ex-victims of their children, I wonder if we would be waved off and told how unreasonable we were? I wonder if any of these decisions were made by a certain teacher, principal, and school trustee? Well, who ever made them; we were going to let them know the mistake was theirs.

The rest of this had very little to do with what the actual fact of us being there was. This story is about our teacher. She had just graduated teaching college and in retrospect, was not much older than the oldest of us. We were in what could be loosely labelled as junior high, but back then had no real designation for where or even what we were.

When she first came into class, she came in wearing slacks, white shirt, sensible shoes, and her hair up in a tight bun at the back of her head. Because of a vision impairment that would not be diagnosed until much later in my life, I had to set the front row centre of the class. As it turned out later to be a much envied and even sought after position and I would have some of the most vicious fights of my life just trying to keep my seat in the class. There were two motivations to keep this position. The first, but by far the least, was that I truly enjoyed the lesson content that was taught at this level of school, and the most important was the crush I had on our very pretty and very young teacher. Of course, I realized how intelligent she was, but honestly, for me that was only icing on the cake.

At first, we had very little sympathy for our young mentor and would torment her horribly. There were several times that we had her in tears or leaving the room in angry confusion. At the time, this made me feel bad, but I would never admit it to my peers. As a matter of fact, I would help and do my part to facilitate the plans that were hatched against her to cause her discomfort. As I continued the charade, I started feeling more sympathy for our young teacher and actually started seeing her as we were. Set aside, thrown away and hopefully forgotten. This all changed one day and our object of torment, the teacher on the other side, actually learned how to grab our attentions, keep us focused and with hard work and femininity, won some of us over and turned us around.

One morning as I was sitting through one of my many recess detentions, chances found me alone with my teacher in the classroom. As I was a bus student, I could not serve detentions after class as some of my classmates did. I could not be kept after class, as I would miss my bus. So, I would serve my detentions during lunch and recess. This was actually a trick that I had learned to get out of being picked on and having to fight my way through recess.

I sat reading or doing homework so that I would not have to take it home with me, another benefit of during school detentions, I glanced up to see the deep brown eyes of our teacher fixed on me with a perplexed expression. Without noticing, I immediately became entrapped and mesmerized within these twin pools that resided in a perfect face. I was dead. Gone. Hopelessly swallowed into some never-never land of unattainable fixation of adolescent hormones. I would have foresworn my soul just to keep her favour and approval.

"Can I ask you a question, David?" Her voice carried a siren quality that left me defenceless.

"Uh, Ya, I guess". I answered with as much acumen as I could.

"All the children here seem smart enough, why are they here and why are the acting so terrible?" she asked with a real interest. At this point I was her unwitting slave. To lie to this Olympian Goddess would turn the soul to dust. So, do I lie? I can't lie to save my life. If I tried, she would see right through me and I would lose face. What if I told her just what I thought? How would she react to it? Would I save face? Would I look like a babbling nerd? Would she laugh? Well, once again I sit being to dumb to run and to scared to fight, so I simply said, "We all feel if we've been pushed aside and no one really gives a care so why should we? They all tell us all the time that we are young adults and we all should know better. We should act our age and we should all try to get along... so, who's trying to get along with us? If when we get beat on and we go and tell someone says no one likes a tattletale. If we fight back and win we are troublemakers. How do we win? Better yet, how do we just get left alone?" All through my diatribe she watched me intently. I knew she was listening, but I had no idea on what she thought. When I stopped, I waited to see how she would react. I waited for her to tell me that I was unreasonable, that in order for people to like me I would have to treat them better. And it took more of a man to walk away from a fight than to stand up and fight back. This was one that always got to me.

"Really?" She said without breaking eye contact.

"Do you think it takes more of a man to walk away from a fight than it does to stand up and fight?" I asked with as much nonchalance as I could muster.

"Not if there is something worthwhile fighting for", she said without hesitation. This answer coming from a teacher astounded me.

"How about someone wanting to fight you just to prove they can take you?" This was now getting interesting.

"If someone tries to beat you up and you fight back, that's self-defence and it's your right by law to defend yourself".

"How about if it's the superintendents kid?" I asked in a lowered voice.

At this point she sat back with a look of deep thought on her face. She looked at me for the tell tale traces of a lie and seeing none said, "Thank you for telling me the truth. Hearing things this way gives me a different insight to the whole situation. David, do you see yourself as an adult?"

This was something I had to think about. "Yes. I do. I may be young, but I still see things that I should have say in".

"Can you give me an example of what you mean? I'm not sure I follow you".

"Well, this is the 60's but people not more than 50 years ago left home at 10, started working at 11, and were married with kids at 16. Why am I so different now? Why should I not have the same rights to decide where or what I'm doing now?" I was really starting to get into this. "If some kid at 16 could be a father then, why are they telling me at 1 and ½ years

younger that I should not even date or have anything to do with girls in…"
I almost said it. I almost used the sex word. I did not have a mirror, but I
could feel my face slowly flush crimson and then turn white when I looked
at her and I could tell that she knew exactly what I was going to say. She
hid it like a trooper.

"I think I know what you mean and I agree. So, how do think it should
be handled", she said covering the faint smile as she talked. I shrugged my
shoulders and said nothing. I had already talked too much. I felt like an
idiot and was sure she thought the same.

"Thank you for talking to me", and for the rest of the day seemed to
say little and gave us self-study assignments. She spent the rest of the day
deep in thought and I figured for sure she was going to embarrass me in
front of a crowd or something of the like. It was Friday and I would have
the weekend to compose my self and muster a defence for Monday. Little
did I know that my indiscretion was totally safe and probably a predictor
that caused a change in my view of education.

Monday morning came around and the thought of what had happened
the previous Friday diminished somewhat with the passing of the weekend.
Everyone arrived in class with half built horror stories in their minds
awaiting the final touches to bring them to fruition. We all sat in our seats
with the air of expectation, but we didn't count on what would happen
next. We not only were not expecting it, we were lost in what happened
never to return to our previous manipulations. When our teacher entered
the classroom, we all followed her path with wide-eyed, slack mouthed
amazement. It was she, but a very different looking she. The bun, which
held her hair, was gone. Over her shoulders and down her back fell generous
and full chestnut tresses that reached almost to her waist. She wore a white
blouse similar to her accustom wear, with one small difference. Each time
she walked in front of a window, it vanished. Continuing down, she wore
a pleated skirt that ended at he mid-thigh and seemed to be held by a wide
leather belt. Continuing down past the exquisitely shaped legs ending in
a pair of calf high boots that exquisitely heightened their appearance.
Her cherubic face was framed by a pair of wire framed 'granny' glasses
that seemed to ride over a perfectly shaped nose and all this over a pair of

full lips that were impossibly red and incredibly perfect. At this point, I realized that I would not only dedicate myself to this lovely creature, but I was hopelessly in love with her. I was spell bound. To top the rest off, she passed her regular place behind her desk and with little effort raised herself to a seated position on the front of her desk. Her skirt slid slightly up those magnificent thighs and threatened to expose what lay beneath. My eyes traveled up to stare into those deep dark pools of hidden promise and I realized that she was looking straight at me.

"Thank you," she said quietly. Once again my face must have turned crimson. She looked away from me and said to the class, "Okay, will everybody take out your Geography books and turn to page 27, please?" One could have heard a pin drop. "Is there a problem?" Slowly the room was invaded by the sound of books being produced from within their storage places. There was little or no disturbance for the rest of the morning. At first break, a large boy named Bill came up to me, crossed his arms, planted his feet, looked at me and said, "I think that I should sit in your desk. Just so I could see better."

"Get glasses", I returned without hesitation. Bill was a big guy and used to getting his way with the other kids.

"Wha… What did you say to me shit-head?"

"If you don't hear so good, maybe you should wash the shit out of your ears? You do know what water's for don'tcha… asshole?" He stood staring at me just for a few seconds, Fatal for him, opportune for me. I knew that I would not be able to take Bill easily in a fight unless I showed some initiative and grabbed the ball when it showed. I shifted forwards, grabbed Bill by the lapels on his denim jacket, and drove my knee into his unprotected groin. A move that I had learned from my father that was an improvisation on a kicking technique that I had learned from Kato previously. A kick in close was not much good, but the knee was a good way to shorten the technique effectively. Bill was a big boy, but went down when hit right. I was mid point of congratulating myself when Bills right fist came with flush contact on the side of my head. It was pure instinct that kept my feet under me as I let go a left hook and a wild right cross that somehow with luck found good targets. Even with the fight gone mostly out of him, Bill was a survivor. The fight wasn't over until he was lying in the dirt and I had sustained considerable injury in attaining that. He still would not give up. The best that I could hope for was a draw. "I'm not moving. No matter what, understand?" He must have understood, for he just looked at me with a glint of menace in his eyes and walked away. This was not the last time that I defended my seat in such a way, but the fights were always more decisive and I don't remember having ever received so much injury in a fight.

After this fight with Bill, my reputation among my peers was determined. I had just taken down the toughest kid in class. It seemed now that I inherited this dubious position. This was of course, not without its drawbacks. If I held the position, I would have to defend. If I lost, the winner would not only assume the mantle, but also the benefits that went with it. This would mean my front row centre desk. This year I fought what seemed to be seven days a week and twice on Sundays. I would not surrender and sometimes when it seemed that a person was after my position, I would take the initiative and bring the battle to them. This was something that was out of character for the most of us, and further help cement my reputation as a fighter.

One day, I was called to see the principle about the fights that I was constantly getting into. This usually happened with you waiting by yourself in an outer office waiting for this man to be done with more "important" things to give you the leftover time that someone like you deserved. It also had a deepening psychological effect and would have you ready to die once you walked in the office. This time was the same with one exception, She showed up. She walked into the office, looked at me and asked, "Why are you hear David?"

"I was fighting on the school grounds," I answered simply.

"With who?" She asked. I gave her the kids name and she watched me as I gave my dissertation to what happened. Then she did something that I thought was ballsy even for her. She stopped at the door, rapped a couple of times, and walked into the principles office. "Where's the other kid?" She asked in none to gentle tones.

"Who?" The principal asked, stunned.

"The other kid who was fighting," She continued in the same voice.

"Well… I don't think…" That was as fare as he got.

"That's right Sam, you don't think! What you were going to do is punish this boy and let the other go unpunished, right? Not this time. I know what happened. Did you ask? Did you get the other kids story? Did you find out how it started?"

"Well… I … uh…" he stammered, not quite knowing how to react.

"My, my Sam, I can see you really put some thought into this problem. You just thought that because it was one of my students that he was of course guilty, right? He was the troublemaker, right? Well, just because the other kids mother plays bridge with your wife, it doesn't mean that he was not at fault. The other kid started it Sam. The other … little angel told David that he stunk like an Indian. Although the little angel didn't know that David's mother is part American Indian, it didn't occur to the little angel that David might take offence to the racism as well as the slur on the family by stating that they all stunk because of their heritage! If this little angel doesn't want to get a punch in the nose, maybe a lesson in manners is in order. If anyone needs to apologize, it without a doubt is your little angel!" I sat in my seat, mesmerized by the passion this beautiful creature was roused to on my account. At that moment, if she would have told me to jump out the window, I would have leaped headlong through the plate glass window without a pause.

"Sam", she continued, "I expect to see this other kid do a detention. David will go back to class now as he has missed enough of today's lesson." She turned to me and said, "David, back to class now. Copy the notes on the board." She added as I leapt to do her bidding.

Well the other kid did not get a detention, but neither did I. When I look back on this all, I have only had a few teachers that ever stood up for me to someone like the principal. The year continued on and so did I. This was one of the most significant years of my life. I learned that there was something more important than my pride. It was my self-worth. I also learned that Passion was the way that one reacted to a true wrong and not an imagined offence. And I learned that if something were worth fighting for, a true man would never walk away. She taught me that.

TEST BY FIRE

How does one account for the various things that happen in ones life? Kismet… Karma… fate? The easy way to do these things is by choosing whatever philosophical school of thought that may apply to the situation to explain with the least amount of thought that is necessary and even possibly remove you far as can be from any culpability that is possible. Into everyone's life a little rain must fall. So did it do on this day. It came down in buckets, sheets, or whatever applicable metaphors you can muster to apply to the horror story that you will hear now. I have no real idea how many of these movies I have watched in my lifetime, but the difference is this one happened to me and it is true.

As usual it starts out like so many episodes in my life have started, normally. It was a normal Friday night, in a normal setting, with normal people all around me. This of course was my first mistake. Normal people. This is a term that by itself defies definition. We use this term incorrectly almost incessantly. What frame of reference does one refer to in the time of statement? I'm sure that Hannibal Lectors frame of reference differs slightly from most. But I do digress. Please leave it to understand that I figured that I was within the bounds of my reference of normal people.

There were several of us hanging around a friends place wondering what there was to do on this particular Friday evening, when my friends mother came into the room and asked if there was anyone that wanted to baby-sit.

"Sharon will pay someone $20.00 to sit until the bars out tonight. Who wants to?" The Mom asked.

"I'm not watchin' no brats", my friend shot back, "Ask one of the girls,"

"I can't 'cause that crazy old Smith is after Sharon agin' and won't stay away only when Ted's there and Sharon's afraid that Smith will come when their gone and do somethin' to the kids."

Every once in a great while I step into things that I do not know the genesis of and spend the rest of my involvement regretting my impulsivity. Usually accepting a sitting job was not high on the list of high-risk situations to be leery of so in a moment of madness I said, "I'll do it. I could use the money and I'm big enough to call the cops in case Smith comes around." What the hell did I know? Who the hell was this smith guy to me or anyone else? Besides, twenty bucks was a lot of cash to a kid. Freddy Kruger move over. I was about to find out. The kid turned to me and said, "If he comes around just slap him and send him away. Hell, you could handle him no problem Dave." This should have told me just where everything was going, but live and learn.

The next few hours went by as expected with no ruffles to disturb the scene around me and possibly give clue to the coming calamity. I was expected to show up at about 8:00 p.m. so I had some time to kill. I went to the pool hall and hung with my usual cronies, but was loath to tell them what I had planned for the evening. Didn't want to tell them I had a babysitting job. I could just imagine the sneers and jeers that would bring. After all, I had a rep to protect. I was one of the tough kids on the block and tough kids don't baby-sit.

I made my excuses and headed off to my rendezvous with destiny. Little did I know that this night would be like one of the experiences that would forever change the direction of my life. Of course, if you did know you would be prepared and would probably learn nothing for two reasons. First, you would spend your time in preparation and therefore diminish the impact, and secondly you would build in preconceived notions about the experience so in effect you would truly learn nothing because of your mental meddling. So when you set yourself up for the dull night of T.V.

and babies you don't suspect that Alfred Hitchcock is about to write the next episode of your life.

I arrived at the address and met the children, was given the usual set of instructions, and was told the kids' bedtime. The baby was asleep and wouldn't wake up until after they returned home. Just as they were leaving the lady turned to me and said, "Don't let anyone in you don't know... no matter what they tell you." This last part of the statement caused me pause. Why say that? What could a stranger possibly say to convince me to allow him or her entrance? I gave whatever assurances I thought necessary under the circumstance and bid them a good evening at the back door.

The evening started out to just what I would expect it to be. The only thing of note was the little girl. She had eyes the size of saucers with one of the most interesting colors that I have ever seen. There was a depth there that really shouldn't be in the gaze of a child.

This one was preschool age. The look definitely scared me. I really don't know how to put it in words. At the time, my frame of reference would maybe allow the description of "haunted" or even "hunted", but even these metaphors fell short of a true naming. It wasn't until much later in my life that I learned about a Japanese word that would put into place my wonderment of those perfect and at the same time horrific eyes. Don't get me wrong; it was not the child that chilled one. It was what these eyes must have beheld that gave one moment for pause.

In my later life, in my study of the martial arts, I came across a name for this condition. It was found in the ancient war journals and the name was given to the most seasoned warriors that had survived the slaughter of the killing fields and had dedicated their lives to the endless slaughter and death that was their karma. The name for the life/death eyes was... shishogan.

Do not look upon this as a digression. See it as I seen it. I myself was the innocent and this child was more prepared for life's catastrophes than I was and I thought I was fairly worldly. Without these forays into other areas of my life, I do not know how I would be able to explain my understanding of the events in my life. I obviously didn't have the tools then and for most of anyone's life is a search to make sense of the things you've already found. How's that for circular reasoning? Now I do digress.

Throughout the evening this child's eyes would find me and study me with what seemed to be a mild interest. As with anything, a person becomes used to conditions around him and begins to accept things as they are. The looks were put off more to childlike curiosity and became bearable to meet on occasion if one did not concentrate on them too long.

As the evening wore on, the children started to doze and the little boy fell asleep. He slept with the abandon of most children, but the little girl just lay on her side staring at me. I kept my eyes focused on the TV and every once and awhile I would glance over to where she lay on the couch. Each time my eyes would meet this unflinching gaze; there was a feeling of mounting trepidation that would not leave me. The once I looked over and the eyes were closed. I let the breath out slowly and it wasn't until that moment that I realized I was holding it. I quietly laughed to myself at being so freaked out by the way a kid looked at me. Oh well, maybe she was just a freaky kid. Yeah, that had to be it. I figured that I would let them sleep awhile and when I woke them up and send them to bed they would be in that semi-conscious dream world that would insure they would drop back off as soon as their heads hit the pillows. The feeling of trepidation passed as the movie programming became later and later. Once in a while I would get up and check the babies room and listened for the quiet rhythmical breathing that I had come to expect from a sleeping infant. The street lamp on the front street cast a white glow through the window and onto the baby's crib that gave just enough light to see the quietly sleeping infant. As I eased the door closed and headed back to my chair in front of the television, something came to my senses that seemed to call for my attention. I looked out the back door and seen nothing that would cause me alarm. I closed the door, locked it and headed back for the living room. Just then there came a nerve jangling sound that shook me to my roots. Shit! It was just the phone. As I tried to still my racing heart, I walked over to the phone, lifted it off the receiver and spoke into the quiet of the receiver. "Hello?" There was nothing there. Only the velvety quiet of the receiver. "Is anyone there?" Still nothing. Then just as I was about to ask who was there, a soft click followed by a dial tone was my only answer. By this time my nerves had settled enough to enable me to react with disgruntled distain at the lack of proper phone etiquette. "Someone probably got a wrong number", I muttered to myself as I moved back to the living room and the relative comfort of my chair. I sat down and waited for the advertisement with the white tornado to finish cleaning the nations kitchens. We were just getting to the part in the movie where Roger Moore, alias 'The Saint', was just about to kick the stuffing out of the bullying bad guy, when there came a sound like a light tapping. At first I put it off to the heaters starting to warm up, but it became too insistent and I finally realized it was someone at the back door. Dam, just when we were coming to a good part in the movie! I got up, moved to the back door, turned on the kitchen light, and just before I opened the door, I remembered the caution that Sharon gave me before she left.

"Hello, Who's there, please?" I called through the door to the late night visitor on the other side.

"Just open the Fucken' door and let me in, Cocksucker!" Was the startling answer from the other side.

"What did you say?" I asked more surprised than miffed. Just then the kitchen window just a few feet from my head exploded inwards with a deafening crash that sent glass flying across the kitchen.

There are few things in life that have rattled me to a point of distraction. This was one of the times that I felt my mortality. There is not a whole hell of a lot that one thinks of at a time like this, but there is a multitude of feelings that seem to happen all at once. Although you are not aware just what these feelings are or seem to be, there are indicators that seem to lend identification to the emotion. Taste for example; I taste copper; ergo, it is either blood or fear. I'm not bleeding so, yup I'm scared. This in all actuality is the understatement of the millennium. Later I'm going to need a forked stick to scoop the lump in my pants out. All this went through my head even before the glass from the shattered window hit the floor.

"The Bitch is in there! I know she's spread out on the bed naked... the Fucken' whore!" Came the insane bellow from outside the door. For some inexplicable reason the thought came to me that I should put my boots on.

I looked down and they were already on. Hey, that was fast! I didn't even realize that I had done this until I thought it would be a good idea. Now, run away… Ya, good idea! Get the hell out of there! First, reasoning.

"Who are you looking for?" I asked in a shaking voice.

"She's in there you son of a bitch! The filthy slut is fucking you right now… the pig! I'm going to kill you, you piece of shit!" came the insane bellow.

Well, whatever the hell I'm getting better be worth it or whatever anyone else is getting at the expense of my life… I hope whoever it is it's worth my life. Piss on it, its' time to leave. The front door seems unoccupied at this time I'll use it. Just as I turned to beat a hasty retreat to the front door, standing in the doorway to the living room was the little girl. She looked at me with those large haunted eyes and said in a small but clear voice, "It's happening again." It slammed into me like a punch in the midsection that all but took my breath away. I can't leave. I cannot leave the children. This has happened before and the little girl was my warning. Jesus! This was a prayer and not profanity on my part. Just where the hell is Simon Templar when you needed him! What the hell do I do next? With either the good sense God gave me or the unerring self-preservation instinct that came from the same place, the front door came to mind. As it did I was surprised at the speed and judgment that was executed as the thought came to mind. Just as I slammed the bolt home on the front door, there came from the other side the sound as if a heavy body had been thrown against it. The small slit window at the top of the door exploded inward as the enraged disembodied voice bellowed its frustration on the other side of the secured door. By this time I was not listening to the obscenities that were screamed from outside or to the horrible descriptions of what would happen if ever this entity gained entrance. I sat with my back against the door wondering were the next assault would take place. The two children sat on the couch watching me with a seeming detachment as wondering what I would do next. The little boy changed his glance to the door that exited the living room to where the baby slept. A chill went through my body and my heart skipped a beat as my minds eye envisioned the baby's crib just below the front street window. With a scramble brought by panic,

I launched myself into the baby's room placing my body between the crib and the window as I reached into the crib and pulled the baby to me. Just as I pulled the infant close to me, the window behind me shattered and flew inwards showering me with shards of broken glass. Keeping my back to the window, I inched out of the room keeping the still sleeping infant against my chest. I felt rather than seen the pieces of the broken window slide to the floor as I worked my way to the door keeping my back to the window. I went to the couch where the other two children sat and lowered the sleeping infant to the couch between them. What the hell do I do now? Just about that time the common sense mode started to kick in and give my jangling instincts some rest. It was just a matter of time before this creature outside the house made his way inside to where I had my doubts on my ability to protect these children at that point. I had to get help. If I could get to the police... of course... the phone! The simple realization hit me with a sense of relief that was overwhelming, to say the least. My heart was pounding in my ears as I picked up the phone and with a trembling hand dialled the number of the R.C.M.P. detachment. My relief to hear the feminine voice on the other end was like splashing warm water on frozen hands.

"Hello, RCMP town, how may I help you?" The voice was calm with the confidence of its' position.

"Hi... we need help in a bad way," I blurted out to the voice on the other end.

"How can we help you?" She repeated.

"There is someone trying to break into the house," I stammered out.

"What's your address?" the voice came back. I gave the address along with my name and what I was doing there at this time of night.

"Do you have any idea who this is breaking the windows?" she asked in her matter of fact way.

"Some guy named Smith," I returned.

"Yes, we've had problems there before this. I'm sorry, you see he lives there. It's his house. There seems to be some kind of domestic dispute in progress and I'm sorry, but we don't get involved with domestic disputes."

"Uh… this man is trying to break into the house and says he's going to kill us. Do you understand what I'm telling you here?"

"Who do you think you are asking me that? You little shit! Do you know that he could probably have you arrested for trespassing, you little puke"?

"Look lady, I don't think he lives here anymore or he would have a key, right? So lady… if there is something amiss here, maybe you should send someone down to straighten it out, right"?

"I'm sorry, but we don't get involved in domestic problems". There was a click followed by a dial tone. Shit! Nothing was coming from them, even after putting up with that woman's bad temper. I wonder if she was a cop or the receptionist? Hell, who cares, my problems right now are still pressing.

I sat in the middle of the living room floor thinking about the psycho wandering around the house busting out the windows. He would have to be tall, because the windows were quite a way from the ground. Or maybe he had something to break them out with. As I heard him ranting out in the front of the house he was not breaking windows. Actually, the last one that he broke was out back and making a mental note, I figured he didn't have anymore to break. That, in its own way, was kind of reassuring. There is nothing that sounds quite like breaking glass. The guy out there probably knows that too. That's why he does it, to intimidate those inside. As I was thinking the whole thing through, I started thinking that if this guy got us scared enough, he might attempt to enter the house and then I would have to deal with an adult male while trying to keep the kids safe. He probably thought if he had me scared enough I might be an easy mark. I was a 140 lb 16 year old kid. How the hell was I supposed to deal with an adult male in this kind of a homicidal mood? Well, I had to think of something. Waiting for this guy was driving me nuts. First, I have to figure were he is. I got up and moved as quietly as I could to the kitchen window that was the first to be smashed. I could still hear him screwing around out front babbling and braying. I pulled back the kitchen curtain and with the outside light still on, I got a pretty good look around the outside. On the ground by the foot of the steps was a long handled shovel handle cut off just above where the spade head was. It was about 4 feet long and made of hickory. So that's how the asshole was reaching the windows on the side of the house. When I went back into the living room, the little boy was looking at me as though I had just caught him doing something. The little girl was looking at me with those outrageous eyes and then looked to the broken living room window in the door. From the other side of the door came a crooning voice that at once sounded pitiable and at the same time coaxing, "Common Sammy boy, let old Smith in now O.K.? It's kind of cold out here right now Sammy, please let me in"?

I turned to see the tears forming in the child's eyes as the crooning tones from the other side of the door started to have their effect.

"Come on Sammy, you don't know him. You know me, right? How can some old baby sitter look after you as well as I can? Come on Sammy. Just until your mom comes home, ok?" I looked over at the children sitting on the couch. The little girl was looking at her brother shaking her head negatively as more tears washed over the face of the little boy. With all the emotion that had coursed through me this evening, none were as strong as my heartfelt sympathy for this little boy. Then it hit me. That bloodsucking son of a bitch! He knew there was no one here except the kids and the babysitter. He suspected that someone might be here that would be scared as he bashed out the windows. He knew there would just be kids here, the hang-up phone call was just checking to see if the adults had gone. He figured by this time a kid would have run or called the cops. He knew from past experience that the cops wouldn't do anything, so the baby sitter would run away. That piece of shit! He all but had it pegged. Now, what to do about it? Before, I was scared, now I was just mad. What came to my mind was, piss on it! If I'm going to be slaughtered, I'll go out like a wolf rather than a sheep. If I'm going to be hurt, I might just as well deal a few blows too. It was just a mater of time before he got in anyway. I had to get the odds on my side. I listened to find out where he was. I couldn't make him out, so I went to the front door window. "Hey Mister! Are you out there"? This I yelled trying to keep the tremor out of my voice. I heard him trying to get around to the front of the house in the dark. The idiot knocked the front light out and didn't touch the backlight. So who's to figure a psycho anyway? I sure as hell wasn't qualified. As I heard him making his way to the front, I went to the back door, opened up the door, and stepped out into the cool night air. I was standing at the top of the back steps that were about 3 ft higher than the outside walk. I had figured on this and wanted this as my advantage. I stood with my back to the light so that if he looked at me he would have the glare of the light in his eyes. This could give me the advantage to make it hard to judge my looks and my size. I stood with my left foot more forward than my right. "Hey, mister," I called, "I can't open the front door for you. I think it's stuck. Come around to the back door. It's open already".

"Sure, kid sure, I'll be right there," he said with slurred enthusiasm. This was my last hope. He was drinking if not drunk. My dad had once told me that a man that beat on kids and women were cowards and they usually did it drunk for courage or an excuse. Whether he was right or not in general, he was right on the money tonight. As the man came around the corner, my pulse had hastened to a familiar pattern and the feeling in the pit of my stomach was no longer fear, but the familiar feeling of excitement before a fight. I liked this better. It sure beat the hell out of sitting inside like some scared kid waiting to be beaten. Now, win or lose, I could stand on two feet and fight like a man. Like a man with some control of his destiny, not a victim waiting for the next foot to fall giving the control of my life to some asshole that would abuse it. Just as the man came into view, from the corner of my eye I saw the little girl watching me. God! There was just so much to lose. Just before I lost nerve, the man rounded the corner of the house. What would happen to her if I lost? What would she do? The little boy inside with the baby… what would he do? So, so much to lose.

As I looked down the stairs that lead to the back door, an average man with a balding head came around the corner. He stopped and looked up the stairs at me. His first appraisal appeared to be sufficient, because he turned his head away and looked at his feet only glancing upwards briefly.

"So are you the only one here?" he asked not looking up.

"Yah, just me and the kids," I answered looking straight at him.

"Well, you can go now… I'll wait for Sharon with the kids," he stated, trying to sound dominating.

"Sure," I said, "Come on up and I'll just get my coat and take off, ok?

"OK", he said, and started up the stairs with a little more confidence than he showed at first. As he reached the step that brought his head even with my belt level, I let my left foot slide a little closer to the edge of the stairs and with all the force that I could muster, launched my right booted foot straight into his unprotected throat. As the toe of my boot made contact just below the larynx, I snapped it back decisively and quickly. The reaction was dramatic to say the least. The mans' arms swung around in a hugging grabbing motion that would have trapped my leg had it still been there. Instead, they seemed to rebound off his chest and his hands grabbed quickly for his own throat. Not waiting to see what he was going to do next, as my right foot came back to its place of origin on the landing, I immediately launched it again a little higher to the unprotected face. As the flat sole of the boot made contact with the face just below the nose, I heard the satisfying sound of a meaty smack with the shock coming up the leg to my knee. At that point I knew that I must now press whatever advantage my surprise attack had accomplished. The mans' hands shot quickly to his injured face as he staggered backward and fell full length on the ground at the bottom of the steps. I knew I couldn't hesitate at this time so I pressed my advantage to the full. I dashed down the stairs and raced to the shovel handle that he had discarded in his earlier window-breaking spree. I picked up the handle in a two handed grip, much like a ball player coming to bat. He had rolled over and came up on his hands and knees still choking and spitting wetly on to the ground. Taking careful aim, I let go a home run swing that made full contact with his left elbow. The howl that ensued was something that made my blood run cold and almost stop. I said almost. He had remained on his knees and when the hickory hardwood had made contact with his arm his face dropped back in the dirt and clutched his elbow as he failed to support the upper part of his body with the brace of his arms. He rolled over onto his side still clutching his arm and rolling slightly back and forth as he blubbered incoherently. Twice more I brought the handle down on the affected arm like a log splitter chopping cordwood. As the second blow made a cracking contact, the man let out a tortured bellow, "Nnnnooooo!!!! No more, Please!" Ending in a strained squeal.

"OK! Fine! You piece of dog shit! If I let you up do you promise to fuck off and stay away for the rest of the night?" I asked between pants.

"Yes," he squeaked.

"You'll leave us- the kids alone?" He nodded his assent. As he got up still clutching his injured arm, he looked up at me allowing the backdoor light shine on his face. Around his nose and mouth was bloody mud that had stuck to his face as the left nostril blew a bloody bubble that popped as he struggled to stand. He stood wavering side to side slightly looking me up and down probably measuring the kid standing in front of him with his own weapon as a threat.

"All right, beat it!" I said with all the authority that I could muster. He said nothing, but turned and hobbled down the walk with what seemed more speed than was comfortable or within his capability to handle. I followed him out to the sidewalk on the front street and watched until he had disappeared around the corner. I walked back and viewed the carnage that the man had brought to the house. I walked up the back stairs and into the kitchen with the smashed glass everywhere. As I closed the door, I placed my back against it and as my knees failed me, sunk to the floor with my shoulders still pressed against the door for support. At this point I noticed that I still had the hickory shovel handle in my hands. The fear was diminishing and leaving a strange emptiness in its place. I maintained my grip on the handle to keep my hands from shaking and wondered why my vision was blurring. I wiped my right hand across my eyes and found them wet. I started to laugh at myself as for the first time I noticed I was crying. As I realized it was over, I bent my head against the solid shaft of wood and allowed my shoulders to quake to the gut wrenching sobs that racked my body. I really don't know how long I sat there as the healing tears coursed down my face as the pent up emotion lanced itself and drained from my Childs soul. My first awareness was the featherlike touch of a little hand that brushed away the tears and crooned reassurances in a Childs voice, "it's okay, don't cry. He's gone now, and I know he won't be back tonight." I opened my eyes and came to see the small girl with the light of understanding knowledge in those perfect eyes. A new rush of tears as the small hand pushed aside an errant strand of hair and continued the crooning reassurance. Without any further words, the child placed her hand in mine and pulled me back to the couch where the young boy sat with the now sleeping infant.

I really did not know how long I sat there, but was only peripherally aware that the TV was on, the kids were sleeping, and the little girl lay on the couch with her brother and slept deeply and only the sleep that a child could attain, "the sleep that knits the ravelled sleeve of care." I have no idea were I heard that, for the first time in my life I noticed how people slept. Before the excitement, the kids slept fitfully and lightly. The little girl just closed her eyes. Now, they slept as if exhausted. I know I was. Christ, was I tired! I let my head lay back in the chair and closed my eyes. When I opened them again, there was the familiar 'test pattern' on the TV and the only sound I heard was coming from the kitchen as the back door clicked and started to open. My first thoughts were, "Shit! He's back!" My hickory stick was leaning against my shoulder and as I exploded into the standing position and charged into the kitchen, my mind was a blur. As I came through the kitchen door, I came all but face to face with Sharon as she extracted the key from the lock in the door. My piece of hickory held in a double-handed grip like a baseball player.

"Hey, Mickey Mantle, take it easy," the big man said over Sharon's shoulder, "What the hell happened here."

"Smith came. He smashed all the windows out and then I had to ask him to leave", I said wagging the stick for emphasis.

"I would suppose that he is at the hospital right now getting his arm looked after", I said as a matter of fact.

At a time like this, something happens to whatever the situation was and it all becomes surrealistic, for the lack of a better term, or even dream like. The fee was paid, all questions were asked and answered, and I was on my way. As I walked towards the front street with my piece of hickory over my shoulder, I heard a call from the side of the house, "Hey, Mickey Mantle, hold up a sec", the big man came up to me and without saying anything but "Thanks," said more to me than any and all words that had been spoken that night.

"Sure, anytime," I answered back. I really didn't mean it of course; the last thing that I wanted to repeat was this night at some future time. I walked back to my friends place were I was to spend the night and gave a brief and inadequate description of what happened that night. As I lay ready to sleep, I rebuilt the picture in my minds eye and tried to parallel it to the events that I had given to my friends. It just didn't work. I couldn't tell them of the fear or the emotions or any of the things that would make the whole thing real from my eyes. I sure as hell couldn't tell them I cried. The only ones that knew that were the little girl and I. I just kind of knew that I could trust her with my secret. With a bit of a smile on my face I rolled over and without too much trouble sank into a deep and restful sleep.

Poems

The night that I wrote this poem, I lay in bed fighting a terrible bout of insomnia. I was alone, but my memory went back to times that I was not. I guess it could be 'creature comfort', but it seemed I was much more courageous when there was someone else with me. A poor excuse for arelationship. It seems that all the negative parts of a bad relationship melt away when you're lonely. All the positives about being alone just don't seem to make up for the feeling that 3:00 am brings when you can't sleep and your mind seems to travel to places it would never go in daylight hours. I guess I'm just not as brave as I wish I were. Truth be told, I wonder if many hero's are lonely or feel this way, especially at 3:00 am?

NIGHT

Silence entombs the lonely room
The nightlight burns fever bright
It presses back and holds at bay
The envelope of the night

The night that brings through loneliness
And speeds the tempo's of the mind
Until the shades of sleep come through
And leave the world of real behind

Before the shroud of Morpheus
Carries me off to Plutonian clime
I lay and think about the night
And when I welcomed it in time

When it came with gentle cloak
With sleeping breathe so close and dear
Then I welcomed its velvet touch
When press of warmth was close and near

A gentle touch in innocence
A touch to seek and find
Assurance held that I am near
A sweet caress of sleeping mind

I lay alone in the lonely room
And bathe the walls in evasive light
To think about what's next to come
And longing for the night

I don't think I need to say too much about what was on my mind at the time I wrote this poem. I do not remember where it was that I heard that the two major preoccupations of man are sex and death. It does seem like everyone seems to running headlong after one and trying at all cost to avoid the other. For my part I can truly say that I am not afraid of death. I will try to put it off as long as possible, but the only true fear I have of death is the mortality of the people I love. I've lost too many. Of course, loosing one loved one is too many, but more than one increases the tragedy even more. While I was working on a jobsite one day, I had a conversation about this topic with another tradesman. This person thought me courageous not to fear death. I tried to explain to this individual that courage is not the absence of fear. Quit the opposite. It takes no courage at all to face something you do not fear. The true hero is the one that is scared to death (pardon the pun) of the situation, but does the right thing in spite of that fear. The thought comes to mind of all the young soldiers storming the beaches of Normandy. How terrified they must have been? But they did it anyway and truly defeated one of the most atrocious evils of that century. Whenever I speak to a veteran of that war, the first thing they talk about is how scared they were. When I asked them why they did it, the answer from all of them was the same, "we had to, the Nazi's had to be stopped". Now that friend is courage and every person that ran that beach was and is a true hero.

"There came a pale rider on a pale horse, the name of the horse was pestilence and the name of the rider was death". (Revelations)

THE RIDER

When the Pale Rider comes our way
Our life in twilight reflect
What will we say to the Rider this day
What was our life in respect

Shall we say, "My life was a lark,"?
To make jest at the coming of doom
Or will we embrace the coming of dark
And the stilling of the life weavers loom

Shall we say it was all pure hell
I'm relived to see it at end
Or will we grieve at the coming demise
And pray for the timelines to bend

I reflect on what will come to a pass
As this day draws ever so near
And there are the times I think I should feel
The coppery presence of fear

The absence of fear when I think of this day
Gives me the clue for my part
Of how I'll react to the riders approach
The reaction that comes from the heart

I'll through down the gauntlet, and challenge this wraith
To the battle of its existence or part
And teach the thing the respect that is due
To a stalwart and indomitable heart

I'll not go quietly into that "good night"
I'll fight with all might and my main
To draw one more breathe on this side of life
Before passing to his dark domain

It will not be fear that pushes this fight
But for choice to cross when I wish
To prove that I dictate all my own path
And 'tis I that fills my own dish

And when he wins, as ever he must
He'll remember well whom he met
The memory I want is one of respect
To the time our battle was set

We all will meet him no matter the path
But our meeting shall be all our own
The manner we choose to come to our end
Will say how our life's seeds were sown

If you lived at the edge of the void
Or your life had a timorous bend
What you learned through the council of years
Is all you'll have in the end

From my earliest recollection to the present date, I've always admired this quiet, noble animal. I remember learning about the massive animals that were used to work at the sawmill pulling loads that were impossible to describe in my limited vocabulary. When I started to learn the history of this beast, I found out that these workhorses were actually bread for battle. I have read the books on the knights and warriors that took these horses into battle and how hundreds of these animals bearing knights in armour would charge across a field making the ground quake. I also cannot help but think of the smallish horses that the Spanish brought to the new world that became the forefathers of the famous Mustang that roamed wild on the western plains and supplied the Native American with the gift of travel. For over 10,000 years the North American Natives only depended on dogs to help with the burden. One can only imagine how this new animal that would befriend humans and increase the industry of an entire people were viewed. Totally awesome indeed!

HORSE

Across the reach of the western plain
Well rent by cloven thunder
Came the cut of a single hoof
That ripped the plains asunder

Never before its tread was felt
A new edge brought to cut the soil
To bring this land closer still
And to bind it with its toil

A power from a distant shore
Flew hence its magic wand to weave
To spell this land with beauties grace
A gift bestowed to never leave

For centuries he carried man
Across the world renown
From the frost of Iceland's coast
To set the jewel in the Orient's crown

He carried forth the host of Rome
The Gaul's and Frankish tribes
Cossack cavalry on the Russian steppes
On his back the Templar rides

To the New world he was brought
He carried Spain to the Mayans Gate
And with the people of this land
He formed a pact to its great estate

The meld was perfect, the song was sung
The horse and man entwined
And from this soil the whisperers came
Here man and horse touched soul and mind

If ever before this song was sung
The two transcended natures goals
To bind together their separate fates
And to form an alliance of the souls

For never were they separate
Their fates forever intertwined
And when arrived the cause of man
The horse himself was found aligned

So when we feel the northern plain
With Bison herds a-thunder
Think and feel the might of Horse
That carried man to the age of wonder

If you have already read my story of Cop-Chop, you can understand my allegiance to these animals. This poem is dedicated to all of those animals that we owe so much to and get the least amount of the credit for their participation in taming a land that could just as easily kill a newcomer as it could welcome him. I know that Chop-Chop was a marvellous friend and an exceptional dog to say the least, but the true hero of the northern land is the husky. They have a heritage that is as linked to the north as a spruce tree is to the Boreal forest or rocks are to the tundra. They are apart form their peers and contemporaries in that they will live in a snowdrift, only eat every second day, and prefer their food frozen. They are part feral, but always work with man. They stand at the gulf between civilized man and the wild frozen country that gave rise to their breed. Half way between dog and timber wolves they share neither the wild freedom of the wolf nor the warm cozy fireside that the domesticated dog enjoys. You will never find an animal that enjoys his work as much as these huskies. Thus I have dubbed them "wolf-dogs". This poor attempt at paying tribute to them falls painfully short of what their truly owed.

THE STORY OF DOG

One day God looked at this world and seen that all the inhabitants lived in it together. God then decided if the people were to learn anything on their own, they would have to live apart from the animals. God brought them all together on a great plain and between man and the animals he drew a line in the sand. The line began to grow deeper and wider. All the inhabitants of the earth had seen what God wanted, but just before the chasm widened too far, Dog jumped across the space to forever stand with man.

(A North American Native legend)

Ballad of the Wolf Dog

Down they pull on northern trail
With fang and fur and claw
Digging their way through trackless snow
Gripping the ice with bloodied paw

With hearts the size of the land they live
None complains or asks the prize
The sacrifice is all their lives
Despite the challenges against their size

When comes the time to do the work
With muscle and blood, with might and main
No complaint was ever made
From the canine ranks of the endless pain

They gave their all without a tear
And never asked what we'll be paid
When many times their lives were chips
That the gambler threw when bets were laid

They gave their all and asked no price
And often their lives were savage tales
Of northland trails and bitter cold
Or spending their lives in savage gales

They were there on the trail of '98
And with the company on the Bays cold shores
They pulled explorers to the Northern pole and
From Alaska's points to Newfoundland's shores

Throughout the land did the Wolf dog run
Never following but they lead the way
And many a Chachako's life they saved
Their own life spent for the Devils pay

So when we read our history books
And they name our founders out of hand
Remember the price that the Wolf dog paid
With his savage heart for a savage land

I have always chaffed at the statement "the devil made me do it". Truth is that every time we do something evil, the genesis of the action is born in our own minds, heart, and (dare I say it) soul. We have no one to blame but ourselves. How many times has man committed some atrocity and purged himself in the sanctity of the confessional? How many times has man, once purified in this fashion, gone out and repeated the same atrocity? History is full of this dark testimony. We now have rise of a prevalent evil in the form of the serial killer. So are these people possessed? The truth is that this scourge is a product of our society and mankind in general. I cannot count the number of times that I have listened to criminals pass the blame to others for their transgressions against their fellow man. I have witnessed, all to often, a person blame a victim for the crime. The song, "he/she asked for it" seems to be a favourite concept amongst the transgressors. I know for a fact that some even believe it. I have listened to criminals convicted of domestic violence state that the woman was taking advantage of Canadian Law with the "no tolerance" policy to put them in jail. "She shouldn't have made me mad" or "She started it so she could have me thrown in jail" and my all-time favourite, "I was drunk and I blacked out", anything to absolve themselves of blame. How many centuries has man been able to blame their wrong doings on an entity that seems to be created for just that purpose? When individuals are able to justify in their own mind of how something outside of their control caused them to commit some horrible act, how easy is it for the politician to find some convoluted reason to do the same and lead us into a conflagration that can lead a world to war. Make no mistake, this is where evil lives.

"Here is wisdom. Let him who has understanding calculate the number of the beast, for it is the number of **Man:** His number is 666" (Revelations: 13:18)

EVIL

We look for evil apart from man
Someone to personify
But, the true face of evil
With humankind does lie

Evil is not an entity
That to Satan gives a face
But the truth is in the lot of us
The total human race

We travel the world to seek our fates
For our selves and truth we search
And in our search we see the ways
That evil will besmirch

When Rome took the world renown
And its legions where conquering all
Ask a Roman citizen then
If it was wrong to conquer Gaul

When Charlemagne and the pope of note
Claimed Christendom was here
The Druids and Wicca's were put to death
And for the glory of Christ spread fear

In the name of God and King
The crusades showed the way
To rape and pillage all the land
For the glory of Christ held sway

When he lead the legions of France
To conquer the world at large
Would the French oppose campaigns
When Napoleon took charge

If we had traveled to German soil
When the Third Reich came to be
While asking the people to look
Are we sure that they would see

Throughout America's continents
Through papal industry
From Inca to the Inuit
They faced the same decree

To eradicate the evil one
To express divine command
To purge from all the new recruits
The devilish pagan hand

So when we look for evil friends
Be careful where we look
For atrocities through space and time
We took from our good Book

We look for an evil entity
Someone to curry blame
But evil is something within ourselves
And thus the birth of Yin and Yang

Do not look to these estates
To find where Evil lay
Beware and know within ourselves
That Evil has its say

Once again we come to one of the major preoccupations of man. When someone thinks of death, how many think of the grim reaper, the very personification of death? Much like evil don't you think? Once again we view an all to pervasive situation to separate it and hold it apart from us. Truth is, it is as natural as birth. No way that you can escape it, it just is. Of course, I didn't always think this way. This poem is how I viewed this natural calamity and how I coped with its ever-impending eventuality.

THE SPECTER: DEATH

"Death smiles at all men, all a man can do is smile back". (Marcus Aurilius)

I am strong and stronger still
Of life I live and drink my fill
As I fill my lungs with life's long breathe
It's my only revenge, my revenge on Death

The spectre lurks and waits for me
And I laugh at him and grimace he
For he knows to him that I will come
But I'll come laughing, not like some

But now and then he beats my game
And of those I love he'll draw a name
And in his ledgers he'll make remark
And strike the laughter from my heart

Of widowed women and loved ones gone
A brother dear and friends along
The path of life that I have tread
A path he's turned to the path of dead

"You Bastard!" I will loud decry
And hot the tears will sting my eye
I'll clench my fists till knuckles white
And swear that I'll renew the fight

And fight I will the spectre death
For me he'll come and claim my breath
But when we're done he'll heave a sigh
And be he glad this foes gone by

For no one has fought as hard as me
Against the shades of eternity
For I've seen the gap his will does lea'
Through life's long voyage on life's long sea

ow on the flip side of preoccupations comes love, or dare I say lust? Just what is it that sets the human heart to this shaky endeavour? Many will say that it is the drive to procreate. Is this totally true? The intimacy that one finds with another like-minded individual isn't totally driven by the urge to reproduce. If it is truly the only mitigating factor, how do we explain the gay movement that has taken society by storm? How do we explain the truly bisexual individual? For the longest time as a heterosexual male, I bought into the common theme of the procreation drive. I was very obviously wrong. Now, don't misunderstand me, I remain a heterosexual male, but not to accept the orientations of others would be deaf, dumb, blind, and stupid. When I wrote this poem, I had just gone through a break-up of very long relationship. I felt miserable. I was also feeling extremely sorry for myself and I was virtually wallowing in self-pity. It did cause me to think though. What was I grieving? The relationship was shaky from the onset. It sure as hell was not the procreational drive. Just what was it that I was grieving for? Oh well, time and wisdom (when it's granted to me) will tell.

THE DRUM

Love is strange and stranger still
Is the way that hearts to the Drum beat thrills
How the feeling always gives way to pain
And how you repeat it over again

In your mind you will ever say no
But to this passion all hearts will go
No matter the trouble in your life will fall
Your heart will always answer this call

As I sit here in shear misery
I wonder what next it has for me
I cry and rage that no more will come
But I know full well I march to that drum

The Drum that calls all hearts to life
The Drum that calls forever of strife
Of heart and mind forever to come
Some day will meld, well maybe for some

For me right now, I think I'll mend
And wait for The Drum its message to send
And hope this time a life mate find
Someone I'll love that will return it in kind

truly think that everyone stops at some point in life and asks him/ herself, just where in hell am I going? I've actually done this on several occasions. I think the thing that signifies a true look at life is to define what it is you want out of it. Some truly don't know what they want. Some do know what they want, but don't feel they can achieve it. Some think they know what they want and when it arrives for them they become extremely bitter, because they are not happy with their attainment. Conversely, some think they know what they want and if they fail in attaining it, they once again become extremely bitter and feel like failures. I have known people that just wanted a simple life, a decent job, a wife, children, and a home. And that is all they truly wanted. These seem to me to be the happiest people I know. Simply put, they have received all they feel that life holds for them or all they truly desire. Now, I'm not saying this is a path we should all follow. I feel quite the opposite. The one thing I do know is that everyone should follow the path that makes his or her heart sing.

LIFE'S PATH

When I sit and look at life
And wonder where it goes
I see the poetry of its path
Spelling out simplistic prose

If we watch the path it takes
And see the destination
Why would we not follow suit
And quell our hesitation

I see it clear and know it well
It's there for all to know
I'll set my foot along its path
And see where it will go

This poem came upon me at one of the times that I had stopped for introspective evaluation. I had just entered mid life and I guess I came upon a crisis. Well, from what I have witnessed, most people of my age that stumble into this situation wind up with an inappropriate girl friend, a sports car they really can't afford, and eventually head for a dry-out centre to get by the overindulgence of alcohol and recreational pharmaceuticals. There are something's I just can't seem to get right. What happened to me is I wound up with a university degree, a total change in career, and student loans the size of the national debt. At least the other guy can sell the car and probably has some good stories to go along with the sale. I almost starved to death my first year in university. The theme of the starving student was alive and well embodied in me. I eventually found food banks and soup kitchens. I had to, there were times I went as long as 5 days without food. At the end of my 4th year, I had to drop out the last term and finish by distance education. I had to get back to work. At least I didn't need the dry-out centre, but sometimes I wish I had. Oh well, to each of their own follow form.

LIFE'S STORM

As I sit at the cross roads to life
I wonder where all time has gone,
Curious of what the new day will bring
What is the outcome of dawn?

My answers, I don't know what they'll bring
Or what repercussions would come,
When at last all's in for the count
And what my life is in sum

Many is the year I left slip by
Without a reasoning care
Letting more unchallenged go by
Would that I could ... would I dare?

Now I sit at the midstream of life
Looking were I've been
Battling storm and rapid galore
To continue I'm not really keen

When will there be lakes in my life
Quiet pastures of glass
With time and abundance all around
I look for it now but alas

Sometimes I think about swimming to shore
Or to chuck it and jump in the stream
But to end it all or let it pass by
Only the coward would dream

But now in the river a fork looms ahead
As many in my travels there's been
Should I just let it coast by
And continue on with the stream?

No! I cannot let it go by
It's time the challenge was met
To steer and travel a new coarse of life
And to the source of this wellspring sails set!

The storm of life has tempered me well
For anything I am prepared
To gain in abundance all that can come
And to receive whatever is shared

I'll sit and watch the others go by
Weathering out their own storm
And to feel for each one that goes by
But let each to his own follow form

I know this fork… I know it is mine
I take it without second glance
And as I come to the waters serene
I bid to the others "Bon chance"

But maybe others I've met in the flood
A comrade that's shared in the toil
Will perhaps seek the same council I seek
And together take root in this soil

think that everyone has some kind of fascination for the ocean. We see it as a huge mystery and it seems to take our imaginations to places we would never go without this bountiful stimulation. It seems to have held mankind in its hypnotic sway for countless millennia. It gives mankind the desire to reach beyond the horizon and set off to see what is beyond what we gather from our five senses. My fascination was always truly held in the North Atlantic. I have listened to the stories of merchant seamen, corvette servicemen from the Second World War; I remember talking to a man that was a chief petty officer on a famous Canadian destroyer that had seen service from patrolling the English Channel, was involved in the sinking of the 'Bismarck', and finally finished service in Korea. The stories this retired seaman had were fascinating and only increased my wonder of the ocean. The ocean is with out a doubt the last frontier on our planet. There is so little we still know about her.

WAVES AND TIME

The waves wash upon the shore
All swathed in azure blue
The same waves that washed the rocks
Back when the world was new

The march of time has no effect
On the breast of the endless sea
But the secrets of its memories
Is there for the world to see

The times when man has left the coast
Firm land left far behind
And set his sail for horizons coasts
To see what he could find

The fearless Viking set his sail
To the breast of the Westering Sea
To come at last to Vineland's coast
To the land of the great pine tree

For a thousand years man did seek
The mystery held in the sea
But all he found were the rocks and waves
With her secrets still waiting to see

All through life I have held the age-old questions that plague all mankind who, where, what, why, and when. When I started this poem, I felt it time I try to work with blank verse. These questions that the poem asks are really quite simple, but if they are simple, why are people still asking these questions with really no answers?

DID YOU EVER WONDER

Did you ever wonder who
Will make sense of this insanity
Will discover the cure for cancer
Will end global warming
Will make sense of Disco and Rap

Did you ever wonder where
All the traffic is going
That river actually started
Music will take you
It was you left your pen

Did you ever wonder what
It all means
Their agenda really is
Will happen next
Really made the universe

Did you ever wonder why
Buildings are square
Planets are round
Roads try to be straight
People try to be crooked

Did you ever wonder when
Will wars actually end
Will forests disappear
Will people wake up
Will man will finish what he started

Who are we
Where are we going
What do we want
Why are we going there and
When will we arrive?

There was a time, that for the lack of a better explanation, I chased the dollar bill. I was a tradesman and thoughts that if I worked the "Boom jobs" I would make everything come true in my life. Well, I made good money, 6 digits a year wasn't bad, but the things I held dear and fondest in my memories had little to do with money. I remember Lefty like it was yesterday. I was working on the northern projects and would work 7 days a week for 10 to 16 hours a day. There was nothing else to do especially in the winter with the land locked up in the winter freeze. That's when I met Lefty. The worksite where we were was getting ready for spring and the push to start the massive hydroelectric dam. We would shut down at midday for lunch and the worksite attracted a bunch of Arctic Foxes. One in particular had caught my eye. He was truly beautiful all decked out in snow white fur with a tail that trailed along behind him like a snow white banner. The thing in particular that caught my attention was the way he would run. On closer inspection, I saw that his left forepaw was missing. The first day I seen him, I shared my lunch with him and that started a daily ritual that would go on for months. No matter where I was on the site, Lefty would find me at lunchtime and we would spend it together. This went on for months. One day he didn't come and I really didn't know where he had gone. When you read the poem, remember that the camp was shared by other people and they only seen this little fox as a trophy that was easy to catch because of his handicap. I still miss this little fellow.

LEFTY

Across the snow in winter time
My furry friend did come
He brought with him a magical glow
Which only shines from some

With eyes sharp and movement quick
His looks were bright and sure
He had a tail that was long as he
And all bedecked in snow white fur

His mates they rambled around our camp
All scamper, quick and jump
But my little friend had trouble you see
His left fore paw was just a stump

Someone had wanted his snow white coat
But it was his from birth you see
They set a snare for my little friend
The "shits" would not just let him be

Around the leg of this cute little fox
The cold cruel wire did entwine
It stole his little foot from him
And forever changed his sign

He comes each day to were I work
He's there for lunch each dinner break
I share with him my ham on rye
(I bring lots extra for his sake)

He made my day a worthy thing
We'd ramble away our time
Until it was time to return to work
Then he'd bounce away to his snowy clime

Each day he would draw closer still
Till' from my hand he deigned to eat
His nose and tongue touched my hand
It was velvet soft and oh so neat

My work mate sat and wouldn't breathe
When lefty came and went
He was very good with my little pal
And gladly shared the time we spent

Then one day he didn't come
I wondered why he didn't show
So I left for him the ham on rye
But missed his marker in the snow

The days went by and still no show
Though I kept a watch each day
No one touched his ham on rye
My little friend had gone away

The last day that I went to camp
Before going home for leave
I past a pick up truck I knew
With a tarp that covers the spoil of thieves

From under the tarp in the pick up truck
A snow white tail did spill
When I flipped the tarp from off the tail
For a fateful span my heart stood still

There on the cold bed of the truck
My little friend did lay
But gone from him was that special glow
He had when he came at lunch to play

My heart it beat with a cold cruel rage
My eyes with tears did burn
And went looking for that "Son of a bitch"
To hand to him the same in turn

I march up into the noisy bunk
Where I knew this slime would be
And kicked open the door within
And there on his bed sat he

He looked up at me with a gap faced grin
The idiot offered me a beer
Said I "the fur in your pick up truck
Is about to cost you dear"

Before the smile left his face
My foot replaced the grin
He flew back into the wall
The world for him took an awful spin

The world went red before my eyes
I pummeled him from stem to stern
The squealing, bleeding wreck I left
With his memory my wrath to burn

As I lifted the body of my friend
From the bed of that frozen truck
I noticed just how light was he
And to the wilderness trail I struck

I left my friend on a little knoll
And sat with him a bit
Then gave him up to the starry night
And returned the trail now moonlight lit

I think now and then of my little friend
With sad smile by and by
Of how me and this little fox
Would share a "Ham on Rye"

This is a poem about a cat that I met. Now to most people this would seem an odd way to characterize your association with a cat. Truth is, he wasn't my cat. I really don't think that this cat could really belong to anybody. If anything, he tolerated the presence of humans as a necessary evil. One night in early December, he showed up on my windowsill and decided to spend the winter with me. The person that had had my rooms that I rented (I can't call it an apartment) had left a massive amount of cat food behind as a housewarming present. Although I couldn't eat it (although when I was hungry I considered it) there was easily enough to keep the cat going all winter. He became a welcome guest and would accept very little of my resources. The food was enough. I remember trying to make him a litter box and place it in my bathroom, but this cat always wanted to leave to outside to answer the call to nature, another endearing quality. In what would pass for my living room I only had one chair that would be called comfortable. I never used it so the cat decided, as I wasn't interested, this would become his place. As soon as the spring came and the weather warmed up, he left. I would leave my window open for him and through the spring he would show up now and then, but finally stopped coming altogether. I guess he found a better offer elsewhere. I named him Nevermore after the poem by Edger Allan Poe. It seemed to fit him to a tee.

A TALE OF NEVERMORE

Late one night while I was reading
Reading ancient Tomes of lore
There chanced to be a late night visit
Washed up from nights Plutonian shore

As I sat alone and thinking
Thinking of my Tomes of lore
There came a tapping at my window
'Twas just this and nothing more

As the candle wicked and wallowed
And shadows shivered over roof and wall
Again there came that tap, tap, Tapping
That echoed down through room and hall

A sallow fear my heart did clutch
My hand did numb on the tomes of lore
And I gazed upon the window blackly
'Twas only this and nothing more

As I stared at the Raven blackness
Two large green orbs did implore
For me to open my window widely
And to exit it that Plutonian shore

With timorous hand I did reach
To the catch that bared that nighted shore
And swung open the window widely
As to exit through that blackened door

In there bounded a cat of stature
Like a wisp of mist with the quiet grace
The largest feline that I've encountered
Did exit that Plutonian space

Slowly a chilling thought came to me
Of another night, another shore
When a stately bird came calling
With such a name as 'Nevermore'

And as the chilling thought went through me
A memory dark came back to haunt
Of how some say the soul does travel
From host to host a spirit jaunts

I looked upon the massive feline
With quivering voice I did implore
To query it seemed only proper
So with timorous voice asked "Nevermore?"

With hooded gaze regarding blackly
While in my breast my fear did soar
And with disdainful grin he mocked me
And said, "Meow" and nothing more

At last my fear I put aside
And with my 'guest' I did implore
That he guest with me awhile
Just awhile, but not much more

He came to stay so much longer
Longer than we both had thought
That a guest should press his hosts' good nature
Or a host expects what a guest has sought

We spent our winter days together
And enjoyed each others company
Until the weather warmed to springtime
Came time to part with him and me

He stood beside that blackened portal
That would take him back to that dark shore
He cast a saddened glance toward me
"Meowed" goodbye and nothing more

With a bound he took that portal
Back to where from whence he came
And I wonder if he heard me
When I called for him by that wondrous name

But now I sit with portal open
Upon that lost Plutonian shore
And just wonder what he's doing
But only this and nothing more

In closing this book I would like to state that everything that I have written in this text is based on real life events as close as I can recollect without naming names and pointing out anyone in particular. Names have been changed and/or avoided as not to bring about unnecessary scrutiny or embarrassment. This entire text has been written to share my life with a willing reader and see my perspective of life from an individual that has grown up on the fringes of society. I at the moment enjoy a fairly good life, good job, and have a pretty good plan for life as it continues. I have told these stories to many and they were greeted with mirth, enjoyment, and in some cases tears.

Rather than just leave the poems in the back of the book, I decided to continue with these as a story on their own. The poems are also written at a time long after the last story in the book to let every reader know that my life has always kept an interesting pace. All of the poems were written from experiences of when I had grown to adulthood. In saying this and this book of short stories is met with interest, there are many more stories and there will most definitely be a sequel. Keep your eye out for it.

In all sincerity,

David de Tremaudan